MUSEUM OF
ADVENTURES

Free pass in the name of:

No. 0001

IV-XII
Reg No. 86-33721

LEONARDO
MUSEUM OF
ADVENTURES

This puzzle booklet and foil mirror will help you solve the puzzles and crack the Leonardo da Vinci Code.
Whenever you see one or both of these symbols take out the booklet and/or the mirror.
You will find them in the little envelope in the back cover of the book.

Have fun and good luck!

The Library of Congress Cataloguing-in-Publication data is available; British Library Cataloguing-in-Publication Data: a catalogue record for this book is available from the British Library; Deutsche Bibliothek holds a record of this publication in the Deutsche Nationalbibliografie; detailed bibliographical data can be found under: http://dnb.ddb.de

Prestel books are available worldwide. Please contact your nearest bookseller or one of the addresses below for information concerning your local distributor.

© Prestel Verlag, Munich · Berlin · London · New York 2005

Prestel Verlag
Königinstrasse 9, 80539 Munich
Tel. +49 (89) 38 17 09-0
Fax +49 (89) 38 17 09-35

Prestel Publishing Ltd.
4, Bloomsbury Place, London WC1A 2QA
Tel. +44 (020) 7323-5004
Fax +44 (020) 7636-8004

Prestel Publishing
900 Broadway, Suite 603, New York, NY 10003
Tel. +1 (212) 995-2720; Fax +1 (212) 995-2733

www.prestel.com

Translated from the German by Hannah Sartin
Editorial direction: Victoria Salley
UK/US editions edited by Fawkes Publishing Limited, Twickenham
Design and layout: agenten und freunde, Munich
Origination: w&co MediaServices, Munich
Printing and Binding: Print Consult, Munich

Printed on acid-free paper

ISBN 3-7913-3426-3

Thomas Brezina

MUSEUM OF ADVENTURES

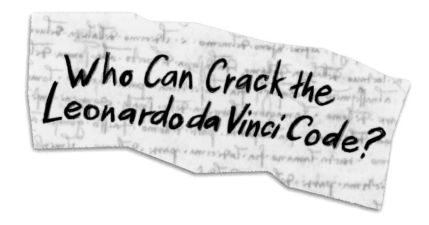

Who Can Crack the Leonardo da Vinci Code?

PRESTEL

WHAT IS THE LEONARDO CODE?

Who's that stony-faced man over there with the pointed chin and the thin, slicked-back hair? He and his companion, a short fat woman, seem to have attached themselves to your class. Have you noticed that his expression hasn't changed throughout the tour of this private museum? He doesn't seem at all interested in anything the owner, Mr. Tonatelli, is saying. His small dark eyes dart around the rooms, taking in the paintings on the walls and paying particular attention to the doors.

"Leonardo da Vinci wasn't just a great artist, but also a very talented musician and inventor!" Mr. Tonatelli explains, throwing his hands in the air as if he could make the artist appear by magic. "The most famous picture in the world, the Mona Lisa, was painted by Leonardo. Even the helicopter was his idea – here, take a look at this drawing!"

Mr. Tonatelli's little dog is following at his heels, his ears pricked up as if he understands every word his master is saying. He looks like he has trodden in some paint – each of his paws is a different colour.

The man with the pointed chin clears his throat and the fat woman in the tight leather jacket raises her eyebrows expectantly.

"Tell us something about the Leonardo Code," the man demands.
Mr Tonatelli's head seems to shrink back into his collar. He looks like a
tortoise under attack.

"The Le... Le... Le... Leonardo Code," he stammers, "What do you mean?"
His voice is a nervous squeak. Is he trying to hide something?

"And what's behind that door?" the man continues, his long index
finger pointing at a green door with a fancy brass handle and no fewer than
four locks.

"Oh nothing, just a storeroom," Mr Tonatelli replies uncomfortably.
Standing protectively with his back to the door, he secretly tries the handle
to make sure it's locked.

The fat woman gives a snort of disbelief. There are beads of sweat on
Mr. Tonatelli's forehead and he quickly wipes them away with his checked
handkerchief. He spreads his arms out like a scarecrow and herds you and
your classmates between the stone pillars of the entrance hall towards the
exit.

"Goodbye, I hope you enjoyed my exhibition. Come again soon!" he says,
bringing the visit to an abrupt end. You stumble down the steps towards the
street and, turning back, you see Mr. Tonatelli trying to hustle the strange
couple out of the museum.

The little dog squeezes between Mr. Tonatelli's baggy trouser legs.

The woman in the leather jacket bends down, bares her teeth and lets out a
threatening growl – she sounds fiercer than a pit-bull terrier. With a terrified
yelp the dog hides behind his master. A satisfied grin spreads across the fat
woman's face. The man with the pointed chin is staring at you.

As your eyes meet, you feel he can see inside your head and read your thoughts. It's a relief when he turns back into the museum and closes the heavy wooden door, which shuts with a loud bang.

School is over for today, so you can go home. Tomorrow your class will discuss the visit to the museum – and Leonardo da Vinci of course.
But why was Mr. Tonatelli so frightened of the strange couple?
From the outside the museum looks quiet and unremarkable, but what is going on behind that massive door?

PABLO

The little dog with the paint-covered paws suddenly appears in front of you. He wags his tail and scratches at your leg. The tag on his collar says he is called Pablo. As soon as you say his name, his tail starts to rotate like a propeller.

He nudges you with his cold, wet nose. There's a brownish piece of paper in his mouth and as you reach out to take it, he drops it into your hand. It's rough and thick, like a piece of card. The words:

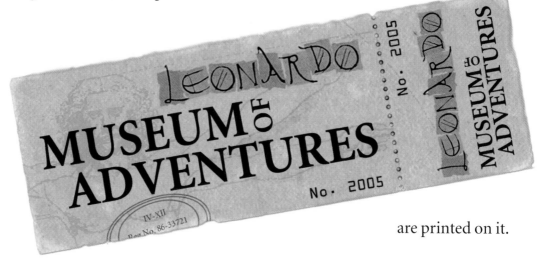

are printed on it.

Your name appears on the card, letter by letter, as if written by an invisible hand. You were on your way home but now you forget about that. The letters on the ticket start to sparkle and glow enticingly. Pablo is heading back to the museum and turns around, barking impatiently, as if he wants you to hurry up. You have no choice but to follow him.

The Adventure Begins

The massive door into the museum is still closed, just as it was when you left. Pablo jumps up the steps, barking excitedly. You stop and take a closer look at the front of the three-storey building. Winged dragons and monstrous gargoyles stare at you from the top of the roof and there's not a sound to be heard.

Did Pablo come to fetch you? And what about this ticket to the **"MUSEUM OF ADVENTURES"**? You've never heard of it before.

Suddenly you hear a strange hissing sound and see a mass of shimmering blue snakes materialising out of the wall above the door. They glare at you and their writhing bodies twist to form the words:

At that moment all the windows burst open!

Someone is waving at you from the window next to the door.

It's the **Mona Lisa**!

Surely her face only exists in a picture that was painted hundreds of years ago, so how has she suddenly come to life?

It's impossible!

A long wing appears from another window.

It reminds you of one of those hang-gliders that people use to fly off mountains, but this one is made of wood and cloth. A second wing appears and you see that they are attached to a boy. He looks like a giant bird. He's balancing on the windowsill, about to jump off. He must be mad! If he falls he'll hit the ground and be badly injured!

A man with long curly grey hair leans out of another window.

"Salaì, who allowed you to enter my forbidden chamber?" he shouts crossly.

"I want to fly Master Leonardo!" comes the reply.

"You're supposed to be stirring the paints!" the man scolds him.

Leonardo? Master Leonardo?

It can't be. It just cannot be. It's simply impossible!

First you see the Mona Lisa waving at you and now you're looking at Leonardo da Vinci. He's been dead for hundreds of years.

"Help!" you hear someone cry from inside the museum.

And then again *"Help!"*

Pablo is standing in front of the door, yelping and scratching at the wood with both paws. Turning towards you he gives another expectant bark. When you don't react he runs down the steps and jumps up at the back of your legs, pushing you towards the door.

10

Come with me! You're needed!

When you turn the handle nothing happens. The door is locked from
the inside. Pablo bounces up and down like a rubber ball,
pointing at the ticket in your hand with his nose.
What are you supposed to do with it?
The dog scratches the door again with his red paw.
Does that mean you should hold the ticket against
the door? You may as well try it.

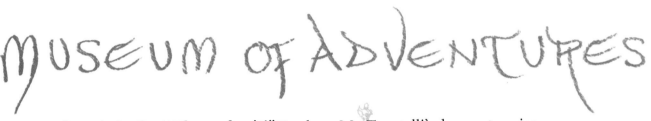

MUSEUM OF ADVENTURES

"Don't do that! Please don't!" You hear Mr. Tonatelli's desperate voice
from inside the building.
Pablo gently nips your calf. What's he trying to tell you?
The ticket isn't a key. Or is it?
As soon as the wavy edge of the ticket touches the metalwork on the door, it
moves! The hinges and joints start to snap and click, then the door flies open
with a loud **bang** to reveal the large entrance hall. Pablo gives a short grunt,
which sounds like "At last!"
He storms ahead fearlessly, his claws clicking on the stone floor.
When he realises that you're not following him, he turns and waggles his
ears, barking insistently.
"Pablo! Help!" cries Mr. Tonatelli from one of the rooms.

You're still standing outside watching the figures in the windows.

A door slams inside the museum and they gradually fade away, until they're nothing but mist. Then you hear a woman's voice,

"The door's staying open, understood!?"

There's a creaking noise.

At once the misty figures regain their colour and shape. What on earth is going on here?

Pablo comes back to get you. He crouches low on his front paws, takes a deep breath, then barks, louder than you've ever heard a dog bark before.

He wants to show you something.

Like a couple of spies you creep into the museum and along the corridor, keeping close to the wall.

Pablo stops and pokes his nose around the doorframe.

You peep into the room.

Mr. Tonatelli is cowering in the furthest corner, clutching his leg with one hand.

In the other he's holding his checked handkerchief wiping the sweat from his face. He's gritting his teeth, obviously in great pain.

The woman in the leather jacket has taken Leonardo's sketch of the helicopter out of its frame and she's holding it in her fingertips.

In her other hand is a silver skull.

She presses a button and, with a hissing sound, a flame shoots from its mouth. It's a lighter. The woman moves the sketch closer and closer to the flame.

"No, you can't do that!" Mr. Tonatelli begs her. "That drawing was done by Leonardo. It's unique and irreplaceable."

The woman doesn't seem to care. She grins, exposing two rows of small, grey teeth.

"What else do you know about the Leonardo Code?"

Her voice is as piercing as a high-speed drill. Mr. Tonatelli doesn't answer. Pablo turns his head towards the green door…

It's open!

You hear voices and you notice a smell of fish coming from the room beyond it. The noise stops and the man with the pointed chin appears in the doorway. He's at least two feet taller than the woman and peers down at Mr. Tonatelli contemptuously. His dark hair is no longer smartly combed back. Thin strands dangle untidily on his forehead.

"Doctor, your hair," the woman murmurs.

He takes out a mirror and comb and quickly slicks his hair back.

"Shall I?" The woman holds the drawing even closer to the flame.

Mr. Tonatelli groans.

"Forget about this idiot, Mrs Bart!" The man's voice is cold. "We have all we need." He takes a piece of paper from the inside pocket of his jacket and reads it quickly.

"I already know how to get back to Leonardo's time. But we're taking the key," he says, turning back into the room behind the green door.

"As you wish, doctor." With a triumphant glance at Mr. Tonatelli, Mrs. Bart drops the drawing, snatches the key from the door and follows Dr. Malfatto.

13

"Your intelligence never ceases to amaze me, doctor," you hear her say sweetly.

The man coughs, obviously charmed. "Stay close to me now, Mrs. Bart."

"With pleasure" she purrs.

You hear them take a few steps, then they stop. There's a short pause.

"Now lean forward," orders the doctor.

There's a short, sharp, sucking sound as if somebody had quickly turned a vacuum cleaner on and off.

What's happening?

Mr. Tonatelli sighs hopelessly. Pablo rushes over to his master, who's still sitting on the floor, and licks his face. You take a few steps into the room.

Mr. Tonatelli raises his head and as he sees you his face lights up.

"So Pablo brought you here!", he says with relief.

"He must think you can help us and Pablo is never wrong."

What is he talking about?

"I can't call the police because I can't allow anyone to discover the secret of my museum!"

What on earth is going on here?

"Shut that green door please!"

As you do, you catch a glimpse of the long gallery behind it. The walls are dark red and portraits of stern-looking men hang in a row.

Although there are no other doors, the gallery is empty.

Mrs. Bart and Dr. Malfatto have disappeared without trace!

But where have they gone?

The Magic Gallery

"Help me get up!" Mr. Tonatelli stretches his hands towards you. He's rather fat and is breathing heavily. "That fat woman pushed me away from the door," he gasps, "And that's how I twisted my ankle." He leans heavily on your shoulder and, with your support, he limps out of the room and along the corridor, back to the entrance hall. You help him through a narrow door into a small office with shelves up to the ceiling. It's crammed with books, boxes, stacks of paper and files. The desk is almost hidden under mountains of paperwork. Behind it there's an old-fashioned safe. It's open. "They forced me to open the safe and hand over the Leonardo Code," Mr. Tonatelli sighs. Then his blue eyes light up.

"They only have a copy though." He squeezes himself awkwardly behind the desk onto a padded swivel chair. With his right hand he feels around under the seat.

What is he doing?

"I have hidden the original here!", he reveals, with a cunning smile, and produces a worn little book, small enough to fit in the palm of your hand. He gives it to you. It has a greasy leather cover and the parchment pages are dry and brittle. ***"It is written down here,"*** he says in a solemn voice.

"These are the seven riddles you have to solve to crack the Leonardo Code."

Pablo jumps onto his owner's lap and curls up like a kitten. Affectionately Mr. Tonatelli tickles him between the ears. Dog and master have something in common: they both smell of oil paint because they are both covered in it.

"Solve the puzzle! You must do it, before Dr. Malfatto and the fat woman. We can't let them open the stone safe."

Your confused expression reminds the museum owner that he still has some explaining to do.

"This museum belonged to my great-grandfather," he begins. "He wanted to open a Museum of Adventures for the public but he never did, and it was he who built the Magic Gallery."

What on earth is the Magic Gallery?

"It's behind the green door. You can travel back in time from that room and meet famous artists in person. All you have to do is find their portraits and stare into their eyes. Hurry up now! *Go and meet Leonardo! That's where you'll find the solutions to the puzzles!"*

It all sounds completely crazy. Still, it could be exciting.

"Pablo will go with you. He's clever and brave and he recognises danger – but he'll run away if it gets too close!" The dog with the paint-covered paws hides his head under the table as if he's ashamed. "He's the best friend you could wish for," Tonatelli adds quickly, which makes Pablo prick up his ears.

"And he's crazy about paint, jellybeans and chocolate." On hearing the word 'chocolate' Pablo yawns happily and licks his lips. Mr. Tonatelli takes three little chocolate buttons from a drawer, one for you, one for Pablo and one for himself. At the same time he hands you something else. It's a little mirror.

"There, that'll be useful to you."

Now you have the little book and the mirror in your hands.

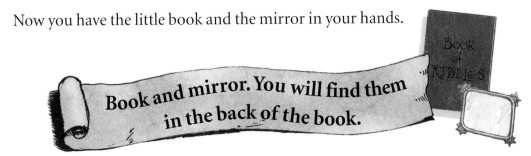

Book and mirror. You will find them in the back of the book.

The booklet contains drawings, sketches and text. It seems to be a notebook, full of writing. But you can't read it.

"Use the mirror!" Mr. Tonatelli says impatiently.

"The famous Leonardo da Vinci wrote hundreds of notebooks like this," he explains. "All in mirror-writing."

Did the book belong to Leonardo da Vinci?

"No, it belonged to my great-grandfather! But there's no time left to explain. You have to go!" Mr. Tonatelli hurries you out of the tiny office.

"Don't forget to shut the green door!" he shouts after you. "Otherwise the Mona Lisa and Leonardo will be looking out of the windows again. Hurry up, you must do it. **You're my last hope!**"

Has anything as crazy as this ever happened to you?

Pablo scrounges another chocolate, then he follows you.

On the way to the Magic Gallery take a look at the booklet and read the first riddle!

BOOK of RIDDLES

What on earth does that mean?

Pablo frowns. Even if he could speak, he wouldn't know the answer. Or would he? You go into the long gallery, shutting the green door behind you. The walls are covered in dark red velvet and the portraits of the artists are framed in gold. There must be a painting of Leonardo in here somewhere.

18

4

5

6

But how are you supposed to go and meet him?

Let's worry about that later!

First of all you have to find the right portrait.

But there aren't any names on the paintings to tell you who's who.

Which is the portrait of the famous Leonardo?

Which of these paintings is a portrait of Leonardo?

Picture number three.

WhO hunTs FOR INTERESTING FACES?

Mr. Tonatelli's voice echoes through the rooms of the museum:
"You have to stare into Leonardo's eyes. Then the journey will begin."
The man in the third painting looks very serious. So that's Leonardo da
Vinci! A man who can do far more than just paint, at least that's what the
riddle says. So what else can he do?

Stare into his eyes,

Into his eyes,

His eyes,

Eyes

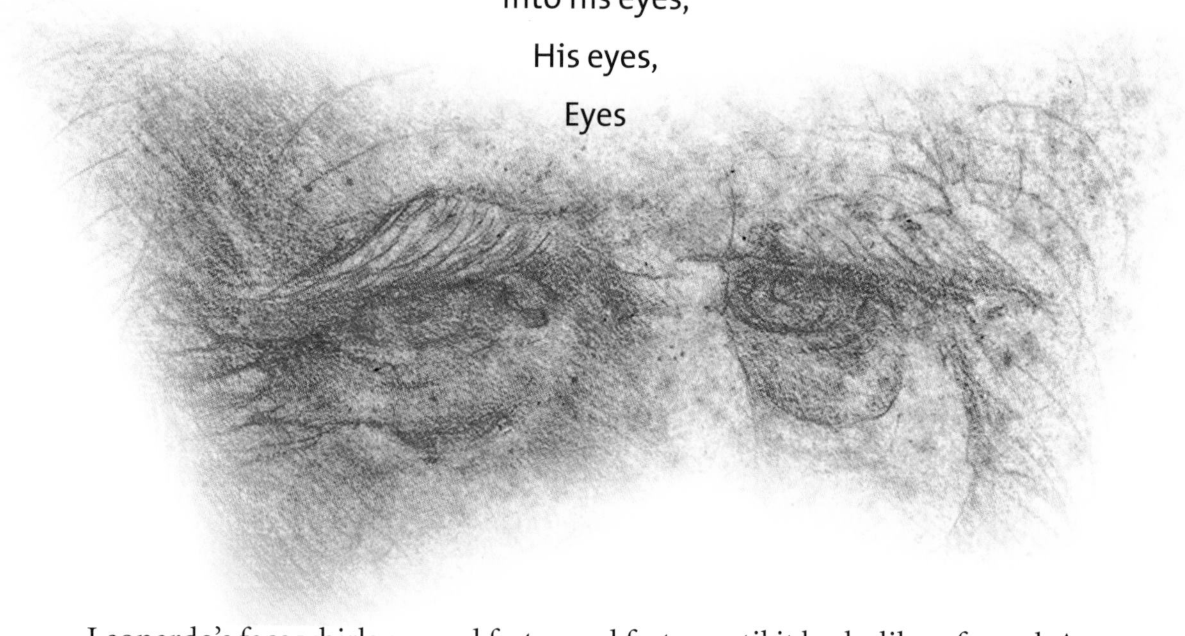

Leonardo's face whirls around faster and faster until it looks like a funnel. A
strong gust of wind hits you in the back and pushes you towards the swirling
picture. You're sucked into it, as if into a tornado. You hear the same strange
noise as when Mrs. Bart and Dr. Malfatto disappeared.

You feel like you're being flung about on a fairground ride. You can't tell which is up or down, left or right, as you are dragged further and further into the picture. A thundering sound fills your ears.

Aaaaaaaaaaaaaaaaaaaaaaaaaaaaaaaaaaaaaaa

Suddenly the thundering stops and you land heavily on all fours. Your nose is full of dust and you sneeze violently. A wagon rumbles past next to you, its wooden wheel narrowly missing your hand. It creaks and groans as if it's about to fall apart.

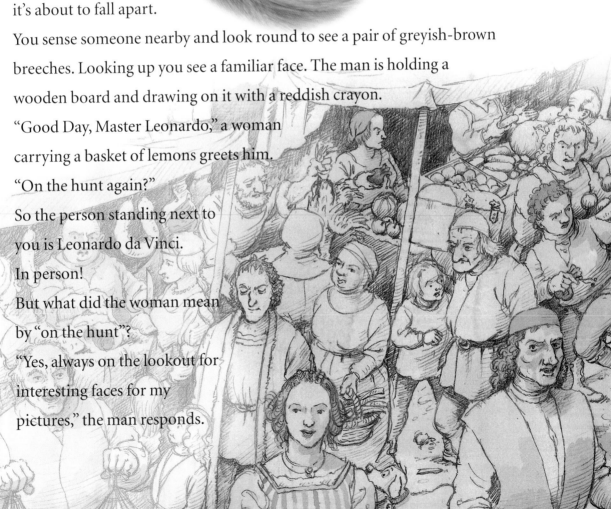

You sense someone nearby and look round to see a pair of greyish-brown breeches. Looking up you see a familiar face. The man is holding a wooden board and drawing on it with a reddish crayon.

"Good Day, Master Leonardo," a woman carrying a basket of lemons greets him. "On the hunt again?"

So the person standing next to you is Leonardo da Vinci. In person!

But what did the woman mean by "on the hunt"?

"Yes, always on the lookout for interesting faces for my pictures," the man responds.

As you clamber to your feet he spots you. "Where did you come from? Did you fall from the sky?" he asks, still sketching.

What is he drawing?

You catch a glimpse of the board. He has stretched a sheet of rough paper across it and is sketching a man, using quick, confident strokes. It must be one of the merchants in the market square, but which one?

Who is Leonardo drawing?

The fish merchant.

WhO WAS LEONARDO?

Pablo nudges you impatiently with his nose. What does he want? He folds his ears in front of his eyes as if he can't believe how slow you are. He swings his head pointing to where Leonardo is sitting. Or rather, where he was sitting.

He has disappeared!

Two more wagons clatter past, one loaded with ripe melons, the other with brightly coloured bales of cloth. The wagon full of melons stops right in front of you. Pablo runs behind it. You hear a short, frightened yelp followed by a deep growl. Slowly he creeps back towards you, crouching down with his bottom in the air. The fur on his back is standing up like a brush. He stares fixedly in front of him.

What has he seen?

Malfatto and Mrs. Bart.

In his grey, double-breasted suit Dr. Malfatto looks like an alien in the market square. People dressed completely differently back in Leonardo's time. Like this:

Malfatto towers above the people in the square.

His head high above the crowd, he peers around, searching for something.

Mrs. Bart's leather jacket is attracting looks of astonishment from the merchants and shoppers. A little embarrassed she fiddles with the seam, murmuring, "Bad leather. Getting tighter and tighter."

Could it be because she eats too much?

"Where is he?" Malfatto's piercing voice calls from above.

"He was there!" Mrs. Bart assures him.

"As he isn't there anymore, your observation is of no use!" Malfatto replies coldly.

"Everyone's staring at us! Shall I give one of them a good thrashing?" Mrs. Bart suggests.

"Have a little more style, Bart," Malfatto tells her, disapprovingly.

Immediately Mrs. Bart straightens her shoulders and sticks out her chin.

"I'm sorry, you're so right, doctor."

Malfatto nods, smiling arrogantly. "It's time we changed our clothes so we don't stand out so much."

"Do you have any money to pay for new clothes?" asks Mrs. Bart.

Dr. Malfatto raises one eyebrow. "I have other things."

What does he mean by that? It sounds dangerous!

Without further comment he turns and follows the wagon loaded with bales of cloth. Mrs. Bart waddles after him.

Pablo looks up at you and with a quick *woof* he trots off in the same direction. What can you do but follow him?

But you don't get far. A wall of dirty, brown leather is in your way.

Looking up, you see a man with an angular face staring at you through

narrowed eyes. The brown leather is his apron and he is a blacksmith.

He carries a heavy hammer in his hands, as if it were a spoon. His nostrils

flare like those of an angry bull. Pablo cowers behind your legs.

"Where are you from?"he demands suspiciously.

"You're dressed very differently to our townspeople!!!!"

What are you supposed to say?

- A portrait in the Museum of Adventures swallowed me up

- We are visiting Master Leonardo!

- I fell from the sky!

What would you say?

Don't annoy the blacksmith, say something that he will
understand. You want to visit Leonardo.

The blacksmith raises his bushy eyebrows in acknowledgement.

"Master Leonardo is a strong man. He can bend a horseshoe with his

bare hands!"

The blacksmith shoulders his hammer and strolls away.

Whew, that was close!

You stretch as tall as you can, trying to spot Malfatto and Mrs. Bart, but they

have vanished in the crowded marketplace. Is that good?

How about asking after Leonardo? The faster you solve the Leonardo Code,

the better.

"Leonardo? Master Leonardo? Such a tall, elegant man, impressive!"

"I know how to decipher his notes without a mirror. Turn the paper the wrong way round and hold it against the light, then read the lines backwards."

"He can even compose and he sings beautifully! He built his favourite instrument in the shape of a horse."

"I'm Salaì and I live with Leonardo. If you give me your shoes, I'll lead you to him."

"Be careful! Salaì is a thief. Goodness knows why Leonardo took him in."

Salaì did really steal something. But who from?

It is the farmer's wife's purse.

THE MASTER'S FAVOURITE INSTRUMENT

On the way to Leonardo's house Salaì keeps throwing a brown leather bag in the air. You hear the muffled jingle of coins as he catches it skilfully.

Someone is following you. Glancing over your shoulder, you recognise the farmer's wife who was selling apples in the market. Her hand swoops down like a bird of prey and she snatches the moneybag from Salaì. With the other hand she grabs his ear.

"I'll tell Master Leonardo!" she threatens him.

Then, looking at you sternly, she adds,

"And I'll tell your parents that you're hanging around with this little thief."

Salaì wriggles, a look of pain on his face. He turns and kicks the woman's shin. Shocked, she lets go of his ear and Salaì runs off as if someone has poked him with a red-hot needle. The farmer's wife is trying to grab your ear instead. It's time to run!

Salaì races through the dark alleys, followed by you and Pablo. He tears round corners, disappears through gateways, climbs over low walls, runs through courtyards with gurgling fountains, until finally he climbs through an open window into a house.

Ouch! Running barefoot through the dusty alleyways and over the stony ground is pretty painful.

You and Pablo follow him and find yourselves in a vaulted room. Although the sun is shining brightly, it's dark and dingy inside.

You're at Leonardo's house! The great master is bent over a desk, working on one of his drawings. Is it a plan? A draft? A sketch? Several more lie on the floor, others on a table. They're all drawings of musical instruments. Some of the instruments he has designed are lying around the room. While you gaze around, fascinated, Salaì nudges you with his knee. "The Master gave each one a lot of thought," he whispers in your ear. Even he is impressed. **"Which is his favourite instrument?"** you whisper to Salaì, but he doesn't answer. He walks towards a drum and reaches for the stick. He's planning to make Leonardo jump.

Pablo jumps up, snatches the drumstick out of Salaì's hand and runs off with it. Naughty little Salaì chases after him.

But now back to the riddle: Which instrument could the puzzle be referring to? Didn't the musician at the market mention something about Leonardo's favourite instrument being the shape of a horse or a wild animal?

Here you will find the solution to the first riddle!

Take a good look at Leonardo in the book of riddles. Study his hands closely. What do you notice?

He drew and wrote with his left hand.

28

The Ancient Stone Safe

"Salaì, what are you up to?" Leonardo calls without looking up. "Have you mixed the paints, like I told you to?"

The word 'paints' makes Pablo just as excited as the word 'chocolate'. He's mad about paint, loves the smell of it and likes to dip his paws in it then jump onto a white canvas. Pablo is the only dog in the world who is a passionate painter. That's why he drops the drumstick immediately and goes to sit quietly at Leonardo's feet, gazing up at him adoringly.

"So who are you?" Leonardo smiles down at the dog with the paint-covered paws. It won't be long before he notices you too. What if he asks where you've come from? What are you going to say?

Someone knocks at the door TAP – TAP – TAP someone with a bony hand!

"Open the door please, Salaì!" Leonardo shouts. But nobody stirs.

Salaì must have gone out again. You can see the door from behind the wide pillar, where you're hiding. With a deep sigh Leonardo gets up and opens the door himself.

Although they're now wearing similar clothes to the people in the market square, you recognise Dr. Malfatto and Mrs. Bart immediately. She is fiddling with her skirt, which is much too small for her.

"Ridiculous design," she complains, "Far too tight!"

"Can I help you?" Leonardo greets them. It's obvious that he wants to get back to his drawing.

"Great Master," Dr. Malfatto addresses him, in a sickly sweet voice. His cold eyes look over Leonardo's shoulder, scanning the room. Although the pillar is wide, it doesn't hide you completely. It's only a matter of time until Dr. Malfatto sees you. What will he do? Will he give you away? Or will he try to get you thrown in prison so you can't cause him any trouble?

Then Mrs. Bart spots you! Her eyes narrow and she digs the doctor in the ribs with her elbow. He bends down and she whispers into his ear.

What are you going to do?

Suddenly the pillar in front of you starts spinning. It doesn't seem to be made of stone any more, but of soft porridge, being whisked at top speed in a blender. It's too late to escape; you're being sucked into the whirlwind. For a few seconds you spin around wildly, as if you were in a washing machine. Thunder roars in your ears, then your feet touch the ground and the noise dies away. The smell of paint, wet clay and burnt wood that was in the air at Leonardo's house is replaced by an intense scent of lemon – some kind of perfumed cleaning fluid.

Incredible!

You are back in the gallery with the gold-framed portraits.
Mr. Tonatelli is standing in front of you, one hand resting on a broom and the other on the portrait of Leonardo. He notices your confusion.

"I could see what was happening to you by looking at the portrait. To get you back, I had to turn it upside down!" he explains. Then he looks down at your feet.

"Where is Pablo?" he asks.

Pablo must be with Leonardo. He's probably still sitting next to him.

"He'll be alright," Mr. Tonatelli reassures you, "He knows how to look after himself. Anyway, what did you find out?"

Quite a lot; you give him the solution to the first riddle.

Mr. Tonatelli nods approvingly. "We'll try that on the stone safe, right now."

Without any further explanation he limps off, using the broom as a crutch. Panting, he leads you to a dark room at the end of the corridor. A bare light bulb dangles from the ceiling. As he switches it on, dust dances in the air. It smells like the inside of a suitcase, which has been left in a cellar for years. In between the stacks of crates and bulging sacks, you spot a grey column, standing on a round table. Something about it makes you freeze – it's like

nothing you've ever seen before. It's made up of stone rings, about as wide as your hand, one on top of the other. The base is a thick stone disc and the top is a sort of pyramid. Symbols, signs, numbers and letters are carved in the rings and filled in with dark paint.

What can it be?

"This also belonged to my great-grandfather!" Mr. Tonatelli wipes the stone column with his handkerchief and steps back as a cloud of dust fills the air. *"It's a kind of safe. We have to solve the Leonardo Code and then adjust the rings."* His finger points to a deep groove in the base and another in the pyramid above it. "Once we have all seven symbols in the right position between these two grooves, the pyramid can be lifted off."

But what is inside?

"My great-grandfather never told anyone. He just called it the Leonardo Treasure."

The dust makes Mr. Tonatelli sneeze.

"I'm afraid it may be something dangerous," he croaks, " Perhaps the plans for some kind of fighting machine. Leonardo invented war machines as well, you know.

A while ago I read in the newspaper, that this Dr. Malfatto has something to do with poisons and invents weapons himself."

Now you understand why Malfatto can't be allowed to solve the code first and open the safe. Mr. Tonatelli drops the broom.

Grasping the bottom ring with both hands he asks, "What shall I set it to?"

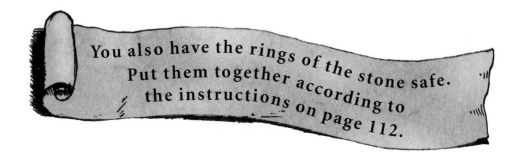

You also have the rings of the stone safe. Put them together according to the instructions on page 112.

It grinds and crunches as he turns the ring. Mr. Tonatelli's face turns red with the strain. "Maybe there's something else in the safe, something precious. We must get it open," he mutters to himself, letting out a deep, anxious sigh. "It may be the last hope for my little museum. I've only got until next week to pay my debts. If I don't, I'll have to leave and the building will be sold." Then Mr. Tonatelli jumps, as if someone had woken him from a dream. "Forget what I just said," he tells you.

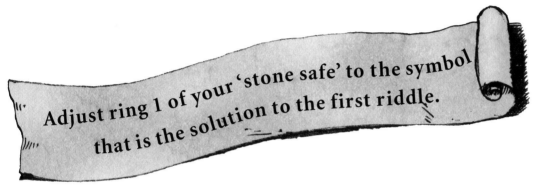

Adjust ring 1 of your 'stone safe' to the symbol that is the solution to the first riddle.

LEONARDO IN DANGER

"*Read the second riddle*" urges Mr. Tonatelli. "*Are you ready to travel back to Leonardo's time again, to solve it?*"

Read the second riddle!

It sounds more like an order than a question. What can you say but **yes**? Mr. Tonatelli accompanies you back to Leonardo's portrait in the gallery. "Now, concentrate on the place I brought you back from," he says.

"It's the only way to get back there."

Again you are sucked into the picture by a whirlwind. It swallows you up and then catapults you out, hundreds of years back in time. Although you still have your eyes closed, you realise straightaway that you've landed in the right place. You can smell the paint.

You feel something rough licking your cheek! What on earth is it?

No need to panic. You're sitting on the uneven wooden floorboards of Leonardo's house with Pablo next to you, wagging his tail like mad. Then you hear Malfatto's voice, as smooth and sweet as honey. "How very interesting! So you're especially fond of this instrument!" he says slyly. You're crouching behind the pillar again, Pablo close by your side. Dr. Malfatto wanders around the vaulted room while Mrs. Bart secretly scribbles something in a notebook.

So, it looks like they've solved the first riddle too.

You hear someone whistling on your right. It's Salaì. His curly head peers around the door and he beckons impatiently, before disappearing into the room beyond.

With Pablo at your heels, you follow him into a wooden barn adjoining the main house. Sunlight filters through the gaps in the planks and your eyes need a bit of time to get used to the dim light. Then you see a huge pair of wings. They're made of wood covered with cloth and Salaì's bare legs are swinging between them. There's something about cloth in the riddle. Could these wings be the answer?

Salaì wriggles his feet happily in your shoes.

"You're a such boring wimp. Always hiding like a mouse!" he complains.

If he only knew!

This winged contraption in the barn is impressive. It looks as if it really could fly, like one of those modern hang-gliders. The enormous wings have lots of leather straps so you can attach them to your shoulders.

"Tonight the Master will be out. He often leaves the house secretly," Salaì whispers in a mysterious tone. "And when he's gone, we'll take off."

What does he mean by that?

You can hear Dr. Malfatto outside.

"Great Master, I'm also very interested in your inventions!"

Naturally he also wants to find the answer to the second riddle. Isn't there any way of stopping him?

Salaì is standing behind the door, peering through a gap in the planks.

"I don't like those two scarecrows," he mutters. You feel the same.

Dr. Malfatto continues, "I'd really like to buy one of your inventions and I am willing to pay a high price."

But Leonardo hesitates and answers evasively, "In that case I'd like to know your name and where you come from."

You can see Malfatto through a knothole. He looks like he's just taken a bite of an unripe lemon. Mrs. Bart is sneaking something out of her skirt pocket.

It's a black handle, with a loop of thick wire attached to it.

She presses a button and blue flashes shoot from the loop with a sharp **buzzzzzzzzz!**

The metallic smell of electricity wafts into the barn.

That must be one of the weapons invented by Malfatto. The two crooks want to give Leonardo an electric shock and knock him unconscious.

Bart has a sly grin on her face. Baring her teeth like a shark, she slowly creeps towards Leonardo. She looks at her boss for approval and he nods, directing her with his eyes.

Just a wink would be enough to make her use that horrid thing.

You must warn Leonardo!

Pablo growls quietly.

That's it. He can help. "Bite her Pablo!"

Unfortunately he doesn't understand your command.

He just cocks his head to one side and gives you a questioning look.

Malfatto is standing dangerously close to Leonardo, who looks uncomfortable.

"So you don't want to show us the plans for your inventions?"

Malfatto's voice is now as sharp as a razor blade.

"Please leave my house, I need to get on with my work," Leonardo insists.

Mrs. Bart is now just two steps behind him. She lifts the weapon up. Go on!

Give Leonardo a warning! Quick! You open the door and shout,

"Master Leonardo, watch out!"

Alarmed, Mrs. Bart turns her head in your direction.

Dr. Malfatto twitches as if someone had cracked a whip.

Leonardo jumps aside and sees the device in Bart's hand.

Even though he's not fully aware of its danger, he realises that these visitors are up to no good. Now Pablo has a chance to prove how brave he is. He barks as deeply and loudly as a bulldog, bares his teeth and then starts growling as if he's getting ready to tear the two crooks to pieces.

They're still standing there, glaring. Malfatto's hands slide into his jacket.
He's probably hiding another weapon in there - one even more dangerous
than Mrs. Bart's. Pablo runs towards them, then jumps up and bites
Mrs. Bart's arm. Cursing, she drops the gadget and tries to shake Pablo off.
Before Malfatto can free his hand from his pocket, Pablo has turned on him
and bitten his ankle hard. The doctor manages to suppress a cry but his face
is twisted with pain.

Hearing the uproar, two men burst through the front door.

"Do you need some help, Master Leonardo?" they shout.

"Outside, Bart!" Dr. Malfatto hisses and limps off.

"You've ruined everything."

"But I only wanted to…" she whines, holding her arm.

"Get out!"

Before they disappear out of the door, Malfatto gives
you an icy look. It hits you like an arrow – it's
obvious that he means you no good.

"Thank you" Leonardo says to the two men, who
nod silently as they take their leave. The artist
closes the door behind them and pushes the bolt to.
Then he turns and looks at you for a long time, saying
nothing. His sharp eyes don't miss a thing.
Pablo sniffs nervously at the thing Mrs. Bart
dropped. You'd better pick it up. When Leonardo
was alive, electricity was still unknown.
This appliance could cause a lot of confusion.

Salaì stands next to you, thrusting out his lower lip.

"We haven't done anything wrong!"

he says defensively.

"What's going on here? Why are you wearing those funny clothes?"

Leonardo asks. He's not trying to interrogate you; he just sounds interested and curious.

You can't tell him the truth. But to please him you say that you want to become a painter and inventor like him.

The great master listens attentively, then he proposes a little deal:

"I'll show you some of my inventions and you give me your clothes. You'll get replacements, of course. I recently bought a new velvet suit for Salaì. He doesn't like it, but it should fit you perfectly."

Why not? That way you might find out the solution to the second riddle.

As you nod in agreement, Leonardo leads you into another room. Pablo trots along next to you, his ears pricked up.

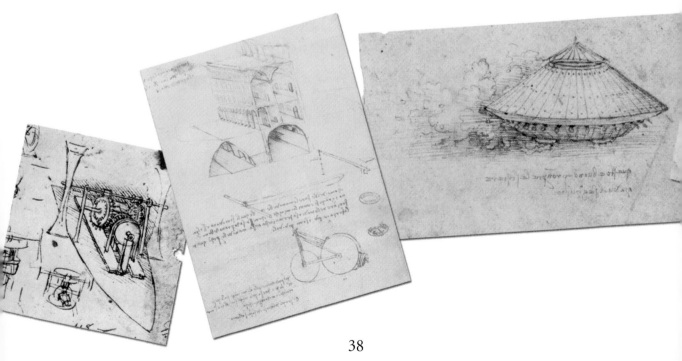

LEONARDO'S INVENTIONS

"A good inventor invents things which seem impossible at the time," Leonardo explains. He talks to you like a colleague.

"Always carry a notebook to write down and sketch all your ideas and observations," he advises you.

You're standing at a large table with a thick wooden top. On it lie many sheets of drawings and sketches. As Leonardo starts showing you his inventions, he is getting very excited. He's really enthusiastic about his ideas.

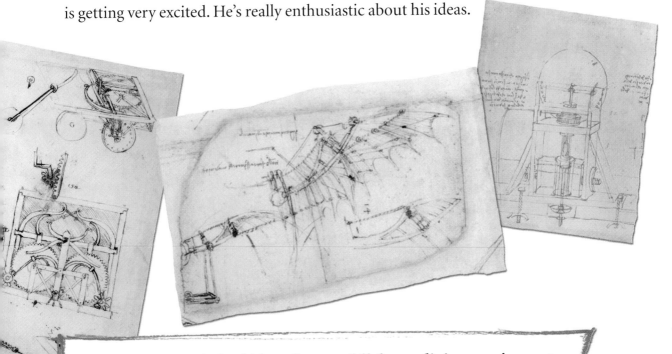

Leonardo already had ideas for a paddleboat, diving-equipment, a submarine and a bike. He even designed a vehicle like a car, which didn't have to be pulled by an animal, as well as war machines such as tanks, mobile forts and weapons.

Why does a man who doesn't eat meat, who loves animals and frees caged birds, invent such cruel fighting machines?

Leonardo doesn't answer at first when you put this question to him. Eventually he responds, "I despise war. But the princes and dukes spend most of their money on wars and very little for peaceful purposes." So Leonardo wanted to impress the princes and dukes, who paid him for his plans.

**Leonardo had all these ideas, but at the time
he didn't have the materials
he would have needed to build them.
Wood was too heavy for flying machines.**

"There should be a machine which will lift us
up into the air using a screw-like device."

"What would allow a man in the air to fall to earth safely?
You need something he can hang from which fills up
with air – made from just cloth and string.
It would have to be large enough to support him."

"Man should be able to fly like a bird.
I want to make wings for people
so they can sail through the air."

40

"This is what a town ought to look like: a place where people can live comfortably. A town where the Black Death won't find any victims and the streets are clean. Underneath the houses there would be pipes and sewers to take away the dirty water. I want to build machines that pump water into houses."

Leonardo had plans for the first road-cleaning machines and sewerage systems. In those days, dirt was simply thrown out of the windows.

If you didn't watch out, you were likely to get the contents of a chamber pot on your head. Machines that could lift and carry water especially fascinated Leonardo. Today we know them as pumps.

The pollution in the towns was one of the main reasons for the outbreak of the plague, also called the Black Death. Leonardo survived the plague twice, but he watched thousands die, and he realised the importance of cleanliness and better housing.

Leonardo had all these ideas, but at the time he didn't have the materials he would have needed to build them. Wood was too heavy for flying machines.

LEONARDO'S SECRET

Salaì is sitting on the edge of the table with his feet dangling down.

Now and again he takes a gulp of water from a jug or crunches a piece of dry bread. Pablo hoovers up the crumbs from the floor. In the little room next to the studio, the light is getting dimmer. The sun has gone down behind the roofs of the town and night is falling.

There's somebody standing at the window!

With a sigh of relief you see that it's not Dr. Malfatto or Mrs. Bart, but a haggard-looking man. Without a word, he stretches his index finger in the air and beckons Leonardo to follow him. You see a sudden change in Master Leonardo. He stops talking in the middle of a sentence and hastily gathers his drawings together. Opening a chest he takes out the red velvet suit he offered you and asks you for your clothes.

"You can sleep in Salaì's room, if you have nowhere else to stay," he says.

Then he puts a few pencils into a pocket of his cloak and picks up a leather-bound book, tied with a leather band. He murmurs a quick goodbye and rushes off.

"At last!" Salaì snarls and jumps off the table. "Every time that potato knocks at the window, the Master leaves in a hurry."

Who is the potato?

"The hooded man with the potato head!" Salaì explains.

But where is Leonardo going? Has he got a secret?

42

Salaì shrugs his shoulders. He has something else in mind.

"You're going to help me!" he tells you. He runs into the barn and pulls out the flying machine.

Compared to modern hang-gliders, Leonardo's machine is very heavy. You wonder if it could fly at all. With great effort you drag it through the narrow alleyways in the moonlight. You're both panting as you reach the top of the hill. "Help me!" Salaì demands.

You are trying to tie the leather straps under his arms, when he grabs you and straps you into it. He's very strong and you can't escape.

There's no point in calling for help as you're all alone on the hill.

Salaì laughs triumphantly because he's tricked you.

Pablo barks as loud as he can and nips Salaì's leg. Salaì yells and manages to shake him off giving you a powerful shove, so you stumble forwards.

Suddenly there is nothing under your feet and you fall like a stone.

The air is whistling in your ears.

Surely you're going to be smashed to pieces on the rocks below!

Heeeeeeeeeeeeeeeeeeelp!

The whistling fades away. Because of the sweat running down your face and into your eyes, the cool night air feels even colder. There's still nothing beneath your feet, but you're not falling any more.

The wooden frames of the wings creak and crack like a branch that is about to break. Then the cloth tears with a sharp **riiiiip**.

The right wing of the flying machine has been pierced by a sharp rock that juts out over the void and you are left hanging helplessly in the air.

"Salaì!" it's Leonardo's voice. "Give us a hand. Hold these poles tight!"

Hands are grasping you from behind. The wood splinters and the flying machine shudders and slides.

"I've got you. Don't worry, I won't let go of you!"

Leonardo's hands grab your arm. It hurts as he drags you back over the edge of the cliff, but who cares? Better to have bruises than broken bones.

Finally you are lying safely on the sandy ground. Behind, you hear a last long riiiiiiiiiiiiiiiiiiiiiiiiiiiiiiiiiiip and then the snapping and splintering of breaking wood. It gets quieter and quieter as the flying machine plunges deep into the crevasse, bouncing off the rocks.

Salaì is standing there with a sheepish grin on his face. He looks like a ghost in the moonlight.

"We'll talk later. Take our guest back home!" Leonardo says harshly.

He seems to be in a hurry and he rushes down the hill in the direction of the town. Halfway down he spins around, shakes his fist in the air and shouts:

"I know you, you little devil! You can't keep a secret from me! Don't forget that Salaì!"

Thank goodness he found out about Salaì's plan. Pablo licks your face and touches you with his nose as you lie on the ground.

You see your shoes in front of your face, with Salaì's skinny legs sticking out of them.

"Do you want to see where the Master is going?" he asks, trying to make friends again.

Go on! Have a look!

Salaì helps you up. "That's a nice suit I let you have. And there's only one hole in it. I still don't like it, though."

What is Leonardo's secret?
Why is nobody allowed to know about it?

Salaì leads you to an ordinary-looking house with small windows. He takes you round the back, to a low door made of rough old wooden planks.

What is in here?

"The Master is always telling me off. Even though he does things which are forbidden himself!" Salaì grumbles. Forbidden things? What could the great Leonardo do that is forbidden? The door is ajar so you push it open. There's a flight of stone steps leading down in front of you. You can just make out the bottom step in the flickering torchlight.

Pablo's nose twitches and his hackles rise. He whimpers and leans against your legs. As you take a step down he starts to bark.

The shutters are flung open and a woman sticks her head out. "Quiet!" she shouts and empties a chamber pot out of the window.

Lucky you weren't standing underneath.

Shhhhhhhhh, Pablo!

Pablo won't calm down, so you'll have to do something – grab him, hold his mouth shut and carry him. He doesn't like it but at least no one will hear you now.

There's a low passageway, running from right to left, as you enter the cellar. The cold air hits you, bringing with it a smell so putrid it takes your breath away. Hold your sleeve over your nose, **Yuk!**

The only other time you've smelt something this disgusting was when the freezer broke down and the meat went off.

There's not a lot to see – just green shimmering walls, tilting inwards slightly. Flames flare up from bowls placed on the ground at regular intervals. Shadows dance across the walls like ghosts.

Here and there water droplets glisten, like tiny piercing eyes. From far along the passageway on the right you hear low voices.

"Nobody must know that I let you in here, Master Leonardo."

"I'm sure no one saw me come in, Lorenzo," Leonardo says, soothingly.

"I'm very grateful that you, as director of the hospital, allow me to come here. There are still so many things I haven't studied yet. The muscles of the arm, which control the ulna and the radius, for instance."

46

Flaming torches light up the end of the passageway. Leonardo and the hooded man are standing over a body lying on a raised stone slab.

"The corpse must be buried tomorrow," the hospital director reminds him, his agitated gestures underlining every word.

Although he was only half listening, Leonardo nods.

What Leonardo is doing was rarely permitted five hundred years ago. He's dissecting a body. That means he cuts it open to look at the shape of the bones and where the organs are situated. Nowadays every medical student has to dissect dead bodies, but in Leonardo's time people were often punished for doing such a thing. Leonardo takes a drawing board and starts sketching.

But wait!

Wasn't there something about the ulna and the radius in the third riddle?

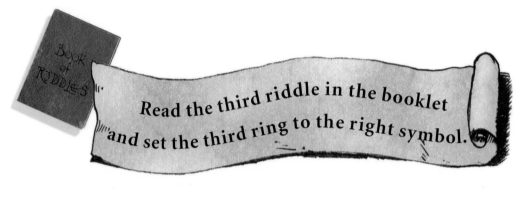

Read the third riddle in the booklet and set the third ring to the right symbol.

CAPTURED

Pablo is struggling in your arms, trying to escape. You'd better not let him go; otherwise he'll bark and give you away. You don't want to get caught down here! Leonardo is already angry enough with Salaì, and who knows how the hospital director will react! He's also involved in something illegal. Pablo is getting more and more agitated.

Salaì gasps and digs you in the ribs – Dr. Malfatto and Mrs. Bart are standing on the steps!

Bart is holding the weapon with the loop and swings it threateningly in your direction. She clearly enjoys the thought of having you under her control. The doctor walks past as if you didn't exist and glances down the passageway. Seeing what Leonardo is doing, he raises his eyebrows triumphantly. Now he knows the answer to the next riddle.

Things don't look good.

You're trapped – the crooks are blocking the exit!

Leonardo has finished now, so he nods

to the hospital director to indicate that he's ready to leave.

Salaì pushes you out of sight into a dark alcove and you listen to

the men's footsteps as they head up the stairs. Malfatto and Bart have

already gone. The two men climb the steep steps in silence. Then the

door creaks shut. You hear the key turn in the lock.

You're locked in! The cellar is quiet. Deathly quiet.

Salaì, normally so cheeky and fearless, leans against you, just like Pablo,

who has finally managed to free his muzzle from your grasp and is

panting fast.

What now? How are you going to get out of here?

Will you have to spend the whole night in the cellar?

The flames in the bowls are dying down. Some of them have already gone

out. The putrid smell nearly takes your breath away.

The darkness is getting thick and oppressive.

Pablo wants to get down. As soon as his feet touch the ground he runs off.

Pablo, stay here!

You hear his claws tapping on the floor as he runs further and further away.

When he barks it sounds very faint. Is he trying to call you?

Should you leave your hiding place?

What if he runs into the room where the corpse is lying?

Salaì is standing as still as a statue.

Impatiently Pablo comes back and paws at your feet.

You're supposed to follow him!

So get out of that alcove.

The passageway seems to be neverending. You go round a couple of bends. It's getting colder and colder.

You see Pablo standing in a shaft of reddish light, happily wagging his tail. It's another staircase!

Salaì, who has been stumbling along behind you, pushes you out of the way and rushes up the steps.

Pablo jumps up, two steps at a time, and you follow him.

Opening the door at the top you find yourselves in a high-ceilinged corridor.

At the far end, you see the stooped figure of the hospital director, his cloak over one arm.

There's a ward full of beds on the left and the air is filled with snores, grunts and sighs. It's nothing like the hospitals we have today.

It looks more like some kind of makeshift camp.

Pablo's sense of direction is superb. He leads you through the dark corridors and out on to the street.

The night breeze is welcoming and at last you are able to take a deep breath.

Well done, Pablo!

LEONARDO'S JOKES

Behind the shutters of the houses, the inhabitants of the town lie sleeping.

Rats run in front of you searching for food.

Is there any chocolate anywhere?

Salaì looks at you as if you had asked him about a seven-eyed monster.

"Choggo-what?" When you try to explain what chocolate looks like and how it tastes you realise you're wasting your time.

Chocolate didn't exist five hundred years ago.

"We'll get ourselves some honey buns," Salaì suggests and licks his lips in anticipation. He stops outside a house, which smells of freshly baked bread, climbs over a wall and disappears.

A dog barks inside the house and Pablo answers. A man's voice starts bellowing. Salaì leaps back over the wall and drops down at your feet.

He waves three buns in the air triumphantly. You start running again, this time to the far side of town. You are gasping for air, Pablo is panting hard. Salaì heads for a derelict shed.

You clamber across the fallen roof tiles towards a steep staircase and follow Salaì as he hurries up the steps on to the roof.

"Right next to the sky," he says dreamily, lying back and looking at the stars.

Pablo thrusts his nose in the air and gives a melodic

"yaaaaaaaaaaaaaaaawl!"

"This is where I hide when I've been naughty and Master Leonardo is angry with me," Salaì explains, tearing off a piece of the sticky honey bun. It's meant for you, but Pablo gets there first and with a quick **snap** he's got the delicious treat in his mouth. Oh well, he's earned it!

"Sometimes Leonardo can be terribly strict," Salaì complains, still chewing. He swallows and quickly takes another bite. "Although he loves to play tricks himself."

What? Salaì must be joking. The famous painter and inventor Leonardo da Vinci wouldn't play tricks. Or would he? Salaì laughs at the bewildered expression on your face. "You don't believe me, huh? But it's true. He told me himself."

The cold night air wafts across your face, but the roof tiles have retained the heat of the day's sunshine and are pleasantly warm against your back.

So what kind of tricks does Leonardo play? Go on, Salaì, give me an example

"Leonardo amazed the priests in the Vatican in Rome by gluing wings and horns onto a lizard. It looked just like a tiny dragon. They all got very excited about it. They thought it was a real monster."

You both have a good laugh about Leonardo's trick. Pablo takes the opportunity to lick the honey off the bun in Salaì's hand. He gazes adoringly at Salaì when he tries to tell him off.

But where are Dr. Malfatto and Mrs. Bart?

The riddles!

You've only solved three of them. There are four more in the book. So what's the next one?

Read the fourth riddle, in the secret notebook.

Salaì listens as you read it out loud. He runs his hands through his unruly hair. Does he have any idea what it means?

"We'll have a look in the Master's studio," he says.

"There are loads of pictures lying around there and even more drawings. Leonardo always does masses of sketches, before he starts painting."

So you set off again and creep through the slumbering town back to Leonardo's house.

All the shutters are closed and the door seems as thick and as strong as a wall. How are you supposed to get in?

"Follow me," Salaì whispers and leads you and Pablo to a large pile of logs, stacked under an overhanging bay window. Salaì carefully pulls a few out to reveal a round hole. The pile creaks and a log falls from the top, narrowly missing Salaì's head. It doesn't seem to be very stable.

"Crawl through!" he says.

He can't be serious.

When you hesitate, Salaì squeezes through the hole himself. First his legs, then his feet – wearing your shoes – disappear inside.

Pablo pokes his head into the hole but immediately pulls it out again.

His pricked ears turn from one side to the other, like antennae.

Tap! Tap! Tap! Tap!

Somebody's coming.

Slow footsteps are coming towards you.

A metallic click!

You and Pablo are crouching in the shadow of the bay window, which hides you like a dark blanket – you hope.

Tap! Tap! Tap! Tap!

A tall, stiff figure with a pointed chin comes round the corner.

Dr. Malfatto! With his long fingers he takes a tiny object out of a shiny tin.

Pablo is trembling with excitement. He probably wants to defend you again.

Hold him tight. You don't want him to reveal your hiding place!

Mrs. Bart appears behind Malfatto, her tight bodice stretched to bursting point.

"Would you like a jellybean, too?"

Malfatto asks, offering her the tin. Now you know why Pablo's shaking.

He's mad about jellybeans. Jammed together, you both crouch next to the log pile. Let's hope Malfatto doesn't notice you.

Mrs. Bart refuses. "No thank you, I'm on a diet."

She sidles up to her boss and looking at him she sighs:

"Oh how I admire your cunning and your genius, doctor."

He accepts the compliment graciously. Can it be true? Does Mrs. Bart admire him? Perhaps she's in love with him!

"Riddle number five leads us into Leonardo's studio" Malfatto tells her.

Riddle five? **Riddle five???**

So Malfatto and Bart have already solved riddle number four! They are beating you. But where did they find the answer? If they want to get into the studio now, presumably they haven't been in there yet. Or have they?

"It's fantastic, the way you solved the fourth riddle without any help! Maybe you'll manage to do it again?" gushes Mrs. Bart.

So Dr. Malfatto knew straight away what the animal was. He must know the painting.

He produces a longish object from his pocket.

Is it a torch? Bart takes a step back and looks at it suspiciously.

"Don't worry, my dear Bart," Malfatto says, obviously amused by her fear. "I certainly won't hurt you with my spark-dagger."

What's a spark-dagger?

Your question is answered immediately.

Malfatto turns the end of the handle and a shimmering blue green blade shoots out.

It's not made of metal, but of glimmering particles of light.

"I bet even the strongest lock couldn't withstand my spark-dagger."

Dr. Malfatto carries the dagger before him like a burning sword as he walks to the front of the house.

You must get in so you can warn Leonardo about these intruders!

You lay on your stomach and crawl through the hole in the log pile.

The smell of sawdust fills your nose and splinters dig into your arms.

Never mind! Just grit your teeth and carry on.

There's a rectangular opening in the wall ahead.

Salaì's face appears, "Hurry up!" he urges.

A horrible noise comes from inside the house.

It sounds like a circular saw ripping through the bodywork of a car.

Pablo has been waiting by your feet, ready to follow you into the house, but now he squeezes past your legs to get to the opening.

The woodpile shudders. One log falls down and the others start to slide.

The first log is already digging into your back.

Then the rest follow. You feel like an elephant is sitting on you.

The air is being squeezed out of your lungs.

Help!

You stretch out your arm and Salaì grabs it.

He's pulling with all his might, but it's too late.

GALLERY OF LIVING PAINTINGS

"Wake up! Please, wake up!"

You must have been unconscious. Your eyelids are heavy and won't open.
Everything is dark and you're still being crushed by the weight of the wood.
Or are you? The pressure eases off, and you hear a faint scratching sound. It
sounds like Pablo's claws on the stone floor. Someone wipes your face and
squeezes your arm. Someone shakes you gently – then again more violently.
Finally someone pinches you hard.

Ouch!

You smell lemon. Through your eyelashes you see a red shimmer, then a
black button with two large holes above it. Damp air blows into your face.
The button is Pablo's nose. He nudges you expectantly.
The log pile has gone. There's nothing crushing you any more.
But your hands and clothes are covered in sawdust.
That proves that you haven't been dreaming.
Now you are lying on the floor of the Magic Gallery and Mr. Tonatelli is
kneeling beside you, trying to help you up.
He brushes away the sawdust with his checked handkerchief, as if you were
a dusty statue.
How did you get back here? Did he bring you back again?
"I was in my office. Must have nodded off," he explains, wiping his face with
the handkerchief.

"Then I heard a scream – really loud and piercing. I hobbled through the museum trying to find out what it was." Breathing heavily, he pulls himself up on the broomstick. "I found you lying here with Pablo on your back." You both stare at Leonardo's portrait. His mouth is wide open!

Did Leonardo scream?

This is just a picture of him. How can it utter a sound?

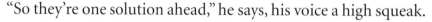

"Have you solved any more riddles?" Tonatelli asks hastily.

You have no choice but to tell him what has happened. Mr. Tonatelli swallows hard, wiping the sweat off his forehead with his free hand.

"So they're one solution ahead," he says, his voice a high squeak.

You have to go back! Malfatto and Bart have broken into Leonardo's house. Before long they'll find the solution to the fifth riddle, too.

You look back at Leonardo's portrait. He's still screaming. No matter how hard you look into his eyes, the magic doesn't work. You can't travel back to his time again.

Have you been beaten? Will Malfatto and Mrs. Bart soon know all the answers and crack the safe?

Mr. Tonatelli seems to be thinking hard – his bushy eyebrows are twitching and he grinds his teeth.

Finally he bangs the broom on the ground. "Follow me!" he orders.

He limps ahead, struggling up the steps to the first floor and, from there, right up into the attic. There he walks towards a heavy cupboard.

He has a bunch of keys jangling on his belt. He chooses one and unlocks the cupboard door.

The lock squeaks as if it hasn't been opened for many years. Behind the door, there's a room. One wall is at an angle and made entirely of glass. The rain has turned it dull and grey. The rest of the walls, are straight. They are completely covered in drawings large and small. In the centre stands a paint-splattered easel. A number of unframed canvasses are leaning against the wall. Tonatelli flicks through them and holds one up. You help him put the painting on the easel.

"It's not a genuine Leonardo," he explains hastily.

"My great-grandfather copied the original – with magic paint – to hang in the *Gallery of Living Paintings.*"

Of course, he notices your astonishment.

What is the Gallery of Living Paintings?

"A couple of days ago I found some notes my great-grandfather made about how to open the gallery."

After a short pause he continues, "My great-grandfather always did a lot of drawings, before he started a painting. Just like Leonardo.

He practised drawing each part of the picture, so the finished painting looked as real as possible.

These initial drawings are called sketches."

He points at the yellowing scraps of paper on the wall.

"We need to find the sketches my great-grandfather did for this painting," he continues.

"Every sketch is marked with a letter. Together, they form a word. We need it to be able to enter the Gallery of Living Paintings."

While you're busy comparing each sketch with the painting, he tells you more about Leonardo.

"Leonardo was very interested in nature – rocks, light and shade, ivy on a tree, leaves, bushes, the arm muscles – he was fascinated by it all. He studied it very carefully and then made sketches. That's why his paintings are so realistic."

What word do the sketches spell out if you put them in the right order?

Here's a clue: it's the name of the town

where Leonardo da Vinci lived and worked.

FLORENCE

TALKING PICTURES

So now you have the word! Off to the Gallery of Living Paintings! It's on the first floor – a red door without a handle, reinforced with wide strips of brass to keep out unwelcome guests. Large oval buttons, each bearing a letter, are set into the doorframe.

Each time you push one you hear the grinding and clicking of a complex system of cogwheels, levers and springs.

You have pressed the last button, but the door remains locked.

Did you choose the wrong word?

Tonatelli grinds his teeth as if he were trying to crush stones into sand in his mouth. Pablo trots up, sniffs at the crack underneath the door and forces his nose between the door and the frame. With a tuneful creak the door opens.

Well done, Pablo! The word was right.

Beyond lies a wide gallery with a high ceiling. Massive paintings shine like huge windows onto the world. Tonatelli hobbles awkwardly into the room, still leaning on the broomstick. As he stands in front of the first picture, something incredible happens. The paint seems to turn to liquid then expands into the room, so the image becomes three-dimensional.

The figures in the picture lift their hands and turn their heads. They blink and whisper.

The painting is alive!

Tonatelli turns to the painting on his right. Suddenly, Pablo starts barking. It's an angry, excited yapping that you've never heard before.

Something white and fluffy jumps out of the picture and Pablo immediately starts chasing it. The woman in the painting opens her mouth with astonishment and reaches out, as if to catch the escaped animal.

Pablo runs wildly around the gallery, sniffing in all the corners and barking, as to say: **"I'm here! There's no room for you!"**

"Shut up, Pablo!" Mr. Tonatelli says crossly, but the dog with the paint-covered paws isn't taking any notice.

An animal! The lady in the painting was holding an animal a white, furry animal. As you turn away, the picture returns to normal, except that the lady in the painting is no longer has her fluffy pet in her arms.

But what does the animal look like? Pablo is still chasing it across the hall. There's its shadow!

What kind of animal was the woman was holding in her arms?

It's sure to be the solution to the fourth riddle.

The description fits perfectly. Tonatelli tuts to himself.

"What a fool I am!" he says.

"It's the picture 'Lady with an Ermine'.

Ermine is the answer. I should have thought of that before."

So far, so good!

But you haven't seen the animal properly, so you don't know exactly what it looks like?

At least you're level with Malfatto and Mrs. Bart again. So long as they haven't yet solved the fifth riddle in the meantime! What was it, now?

"Hmmmmmmmmm," Tonatelli says, frowning so his bushy eyebrows almost join together. "I should have thought of the Lady with an Ermine."

Set the animal on the fourth ring.

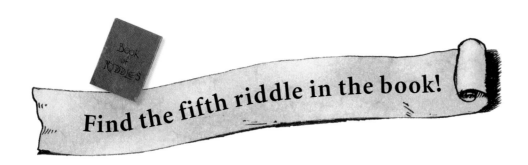

Malfatto obviously knew the painting and that's how he found the solution so quickly.

"I really don't know what's meant by 'drawing-aid'!" Tonatelli confesses dejectedly.

Is there any other way you could return to Leonardo's time?

After hesitating for ages Tonatelli nods reluctantly.

What do you have to do?

Silently Mr. Tonatelli limps out of the gallery. You and Pablo follow him.

"Malfatto has the blue compass!" he mutters.

What's that supposed to mean?

When you reach the ground floor, Mr. Tonatelli takes out a handful of chocolates and shares them between you, Pablo and himself.

This little snack is very welcome. Pablo chases his chocolates around the floor before eating them. Tonatelli hobbles over to a black chest. It is enclosed in a massive iron cage fastened with several heavy padlocks, as if it were a dangerous animal. With much jingling and jangling Tonatelli opens one padlock after another. He even needs several keys just to open the chest. As he lifts the lid, he reveals its fiery-red velvet lining. On it lies a shining, instrument the size and shape of an egg. Carefully he takes it out.

One half of the instrument is made of hammered gold, the other of crystal clear glass.

From within the instrument a warm, golden light glows.

A dark-red precious stone is set into its rounded end and Tonatelli turns it slowly. Through the domed glass you can see a miniature world.

An ancient car is driving round in circles and you can hear it chugging.

A tiny turn of the precious stone is enough to replace the car with a horse-drawn tram, the horse's hooves clip-clopping on the road. The further Tonatelli turns the red stone, the further back in time you go – through knights and Pharaohs right back to cavemen.

"The **red compass** can take you back to Leonardo's time," Tonatelli says slowly, staring at the instrument in his hand. He sets it to the town where you met Leonardo. "But this compass can only take you further into the past – to get back to the present, you need the **blue compass."**

OK! But Malfatto must have got hold of that one; otherwise he'd be stuck in Leonardo's time. Tonatelli certainly wouldn't have brought him back using the painting. The devilish crook has thought of everything!

At first Tonatelli wants to give you the red compass , but then he changes his mind.

"Too dangerous! You'll never be able to get your hands on the blue compass. Malfatto won't let you have it."

Pablo jumps up at Mr. Tonatelli's legs, as if he wants to take a look at the instrument. Although the little dog isn't heavy, he manages to knock his master off balance. Tonatelli falls on top of you, still holding the red compass.

A flash shoots out from the instrument, hotter and more dazzling than the sun. It engulfs you and the ground beneath your feet disappears.

LEONARDO'S TRICKS

"Your tricks! Speak for heavens sake!"

The scene you see before you is appalling.

Leonardo is tied to a chair. Malfatto is standing in front of him, threatening him with the spark-dagger. Mrs. Bart is waving the wire loop, which shoots out blue flashes. She looks like an evil fat fairy. Leonardo is staring at the strangers in amazement.

They have their backs to you and haven't noticed you yet. You, Tonatelli and Pablo have all been catapulted into Leonardo's house. So the **red compass** works. But how are you supposed to get hold of the **blue one**, which Malfatto is holding in his hands?

Tonatelli rolls behind a pile of sacks, holding his injured leg. Pablo darts for cover next to him, and you squeeze yourself in between them. You can see the crooks through the gaps between the sacks.

Malfatto waves the blade of the spark-dagger backwards and forwards in front of the artist's face.

"How do you manage to paint nature so realistically?"

You can hear, by the tone of his voice, that he has repeated this question more than once.

"Who are you?" Leonardo demands, but he gets no answer.

Leonardo is tied up not just with a rope, but also with a thin, shiny cord, making it impossible for the strong man to free himself. You can't help him either.

You are powerless against the spark-dagger and Mrs. Bart's looped weapon.

Malfatto rests his elbow on an easel with a mean smile. He takes the shiny tin out of his pocket and flicks the lid open.

Pablo's sensitive nose picks up the smell of jellybeans straight away. His tail starts wagging automatically as his mouth begins to water.

Thump – thump – thump

his tail beats rhythmically on the floor. Hold him tight; otherwise the noise will give you away!

With a sharp **snap** Malfatto closes the tin. Contempt is written all over his face.

Blue flashes shoot from the looped weapon again.

The crackling is like pinpricks in your ears.

"Shall I start on him?" Bart asks bluntly.

Malfatto stares at Leonardo for a long time.

"No!"

Disappointed, Mrs. Bart lowers the loop with a snort.

"We're leaving, Bart!"

"What?" she asks, "But the riddle…"

"We're leaving!" Malfatto repeats. His voice is as hard as steel.

He turns and marches stiffly out of the studio, leaving Mrs. Bart to follow him.

Pablo creeps after them and signals with a happy yelp that the crooks really have left the house. Where can they be going?

Bang!

A board, which was leaning against the wall, crashes to the floor and Salaì's scruffy head appears from a hole, which must lead to the log pile.

Even in the dim candlelight you can see that his face is deathly pale and his lower lip is trembling. He crawls out and attempts to free Leonardo but the thin cord cuts his fingers when he tries to rip it off.

He grabs a long knife, but even that won't cut it.

"One of Malfatto's dreadful inventions," Mr. Tonatelli growls.

What about Malfatto and Bart? What do they have planned? They still have the **blue compass.**

Salaì's eyes are as wide as saucers when he sees you pop up from behind the sacks. He tries to speak, but all that comes out of his mouth is a confused stammer.

"Can you follow those two, without letting them see you?" you ask him. He gives you a big hug, delighted and relieved that you weren't crushed by the logs.

In fact he nearly crushes you himself as he squeezes all the air from your lungs. You even think you heard a rib crack. Then he dashes off at top speed.

"Try my lighter!" says Tonatelli, giving you a bulky object from the pocket of his corduroy trousers. The flame melts the thin cord and Leonardo is free. With a grateful sigh he stands up and stretches his stiff limbs. He looks at you, then at Mr. Tonatelli, who is heaving himself up from behind the sacks, and then at Pablo.

"The world is full of miracles," he begins, "But the way you appeared and disappeared seems more than a miracle to me. Tell me honestly how you did it!"

Should you tell him?

Mr. Tonatelli gives a quick nod. "But only if you don't make any notes, great Master," he says.

Leonardo, who is about to pick up a notebook, reluctantly withdraws his hand.

Tonatelli whispers in your ear, "Imagine if a researcher from our time were to find an entry in Leonardo's notebook about us and Pablo! How confusing would that be?"

So Tonatelli tells Leonardo about the mysterious safe, the Leonardo Code and the crooks who want to crack it.

"I'll help you," Leonardo promises.

"Read the riddle to him!" Tonatelli tells you.

Leonardo listens attentively. "Paintings of nature look so realistic." He gazes into the distance, as if he could find the solution there. "Come!" The next room is another studio. A large oil painting stands on an easel. It's nearly finished, and shows the Virgin Mary in a cave. "The Virgin of the Rocks," Tonatelli whispers emotionally. "Nobody has ever seen it like this – freshly painted."

"Let me tell you about my observations!" Leonardo begins. "The further away a person, animal, tree or house is, the smaller it seems to be. The rocks in the background are actually the same height as those directly behind the Virgin Mary, but since they are much further away, they appear to be smaller.

Colours, too, change in the distance– the haze fades them and they seem bluer. That's why I painted the rocks in the background blue and not brown. Besides that, things are less sharp the further away they are. They look as if a layer of mist covered them. You can see this with the rocks again – the sharp edges and ridges become more and more blurred." Leonardo uses his hands as he speaks. He pulls an unfinished black and white pain- ting from a pile of can- vasses, and continues: "Look, in this study of a gown you can see how shadows work.

They bring everything to life. The closer the shadow is to an object, the darker it is. The further away it is, the fainter it becomes. Strong sources of light produce dark shadows. On a sunny day shadows look different to those on a cloudy day."

He turns back to the painting of the Virgin of the Rocks and continues:

"You know, it's also very interesting that I only use a few colours – black and white, yellow, blue and red. With these, a painter can mix any shade."

Leonardo becomes quite passionate when he talks about his knowledge and discoveries. Now he reaches for a square object, about the size of a bedside table, which he has wrapped in a cloth. He opens one of the shutters, and the gentle morning light streams into the studio. Leonardo takes a wooden box out of the cloth. There's a small hole on one side, and the opposite side is open. He points the hole at a tree in his garden and covers the area between the window and the box, so the light can only enter through the small hole. The image of the tree appears on the opposite wall. It's upside down, but you can see every branch.

Leonardo covers it with a piece of paper and starts drawing.

"This way, I get the exact shape of the tree!" he explains.

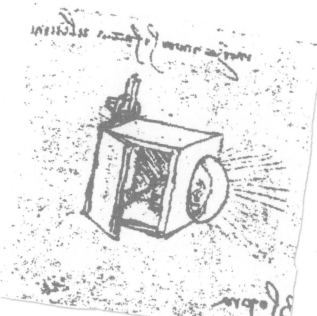

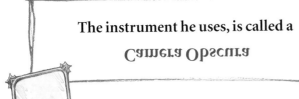

The instrument he uses, is called a
Camera Obscura

The ancestor of the modern
Camera

Now it is obvious how you should set the fifth ring.

LEONARDO'S STUDIO

There are just two more riddles to be solved, then you can crack the Leonardo Code and open the stone safe.

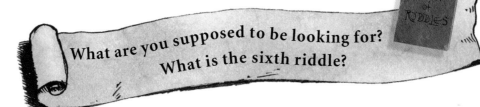

What are you supposed to be looking for?
What is the sixth riddle?

There's a rumbling noise from the studio next door, as if something heavy has fallen over. Leonardo flings the door open and peers into the room.

"Good day, Master Leonardo!" a voice shouts.

"Hello, Alberto! You can get to work right away!" Leonardo replies.

"Would you like to have a little rest?" he asks Mr. Tonatelli,

"You look completely exhausted." Mr. Tonatelli gratefully accepts his offer and Leonardo leads him into a darkened room.

The only thing in it is a simple wooden bed which creaks ominously when the plump man lies down.

You and Pablo accompany Leonardo into the larger studio.

Now you have a chance to look around. Pablo jumps straight into a palette of freshly mixed paints. Using his paws as brushes, he smears the paint onto a whitewashed board leaning against the wall, barking and yelping with joy. Leonardo is fascinated.

"This is the first time I've ever seen a dog paint!" he says, full of admiration.

"It's not quite my style, but his painting shows a certain depth and intensity."

Salaì comes in from outside. His face is dirty and his trousers are torn.

"Salaì, you good-for-nothing!" Leonardo grumbles.

"I can't buy you a new pair of trousers every day." Then, standing in front of a wooden board, he takes a pencil in each hand and starts drawing with both hands at the same time.

So he can also draw and paint with his right hand.

He draws confidently, hardly seeming to think about it. The outline of a woman appears.

"Shouldn't you be sweeping the studio, Salaì?"

Salaì pulls a grumpy face.

"But I was told to follow the thieves who attacked you," he argues.

Leonardo stops drawing for a minute, "Where did they go? What did you see?"

"I followed them to the edge of town" he reports.

"I heard them speaking. They said they wanted to go to sleep, but they didn't say where."

"They suddenly disappeared behind the house with the green roof. I've been running all over town looking for them. My legs are killing me. But I couldn't find them anywhere."

What's that sticky stuff on Salaì's face? Is that honey? Did he steal another honey-bun?

"OK, you can sweep the floor now," orders Leonardo.

"I'm tired!" Salaì moans.

"Well you look fine to me. So you should have enough strength to clean the dust out of the every corner." Grumbling, Salaì picks up the broom and pretends to sweep the room. Just for fun he sticks the broom between your feet, then twists it like a screwdriver so you land on your backside. Leonardo doesn't notice and Salaì quickly carries on pretending to sweep the floor. Leonardo is very untidy. A table and several chairs are overflowing with sketches, sheets of paper, plans and notebooks. He obviously doesn't consider clearing up to be important.

Meanwhile two young men have arrived. They both greet Leonardo with a bow and set to work. One of them is painting a landscape and keeps squinting at it critically. The other, who is a bit older, stands in front of a painting of the Madonna with the infant Jesus. He is painting a stone pillar, but the hands and faces have still to be done.

"The work is ready for you now, Master Leonardo," he says turning towards the great artist.

Didn't Leonardo paint everything himself?

"I'll be there in a moment," Leonardo replies. So he draws things first, then his assistants paint parts of them, and finally he paints the hands and faces of the figures.

Alberto is squatting in a corner in front of a bunch of wilting flowers. Sunlight shines on them through the window.

The young painter leans forward and stares at the flowers, as if he could photograph them with his eyes. So far he's only managed to draw a few tentative lines. Leonardo comes up behind him and lays a hand on his shoulder, "Don't give up, just draw what you see. It's the practice and the study of light and shade that will make you a great artist."

Salaì is behaving suspiciously. There's something strange about him. But what is it?

If he had been running all the time, he should be out of breath.

A PAINTING CRASHES DOWN

The front door slams shut.

The sound echoes through the house like a gunshot. Leonardo, his students and his assistants look up from their work, shocked by the noise.

"The crooks!" Leonardo exclaims. He puts his pencil aside and moves towards the lobby. You, Pablo and Salaì go after him. Pablo's ears are swivelling from left to right. He can hear noises but he doesn't seem to understand what they mean. His nose twitches, but his hackles aren't raised. Yet!

Leonardo orders you three to go back to the studio. Then he beckons to the others to go with him. Armed with large pots of paint, an easel and a wooden bucket, they head for the lobby. Leonardo slams the door behind him. To make sure that you can't follow, he turns the key twice.

Have Malfatto and Mrs. Bart come back?

Cursing loudly, Salaì throws the broom across the room.

Pablo jumps up and tries to catch it, but he misses. The broom flies towards the new painting. Disaster is inevitable.

With a terrible bang the broomstick hits the canvas.

It topples to one side, falls off the easel and lands, painted side down, on the ground.

You all hold your breath.

You hear embarrassed laughter from behind the closed door. It doesn't sound as if Leonardo's men have bumped into Dr. Malfatto.

You hear Leonardo shout, "Take a short break!"

Footsteps shuffle across the wooden floor and chairs are pushed about. Alberto and the two other painters are now sitting in the room next door. But the three of you are still locked in the studio. Pablo sniffs at the painting lying upside down on the floor.

He seems to be thinking, "That smells like trouble."

Leonardo will go mad when he sees this. Salaì takes a deep breath and sidles up to the painting nervously, as if it might jump up and attack him at any moment. He picks it up carefully. At first sight, it looks undamaged.

He utters a sigh of relief. But looking at it closely you discover a white patch where the paint has come off.

"The master is sure to notice," Salaì groans.

You must retouch that area! Mix the paints and have a go!

Salaì points at you and says, "I'll tell Master Leonardo, that you ruined it."

Pablo growls at Salaì trying to sound like a vicious dog.

Salaì raises his arms to protect himself. Even he is scared of Pablo's teeth. He starts to stammer.

"We… we could try… to repair it. I have often watched the master…paint."

He tells you as much as he can remember.

"First of all, you have to prepare the wooden board. So you cover it with a base coat made from a mixture of gypsum and glue. Then you draw the design on the base. The paint is made from a mixture of pigment and oil. Leonardo uses turpentine to dilute the paints, then he brushes on a thin coat. Many layers are painted on top of one another. But wait, sometimes Leonardo also uses other paints. He calls them tempera. For these, he mixes the pigments with egg yolk."

You hear loud voices coming from the lobby. The words are muffled, but you can make out that they're arguing about a painting. The voices die away.

Leonardo will be back soon, and you still haven't repaired the picture.

Hastily Salaì mixes the paint in jars, pots and even in a shell. It's amazing to see which pigments he uses. Leonardo asks the guest to go into the smaller studio, where he demonstrated the 'camera obscura'.

Before you can catch a glimpse of the stranger, he has already shut the connecting door to the studio and locked it, too.

It's a good thing, as Salaì is still busy retouching the painting.

"My Master has been trying to finish it for the last four years!"

Through a knothole in the door you see a man in an elegant robe.

His face is red with fury. His fists are clenched and he hops up and down as he speaks. "When will the work finally be finished?"

Leonardo is not at all bothered by the visitor's anger.

"I'm still looking for the right face," he explains calmly.

"I'm not prepared to use an unsuitable face!"

The guest isn't satisfied with this answer. He keeps on complaining, but Leonardo remains unmoved by his anger.

Salaì puts the painting back on the easel.

"The great Master is always eager to start a new project. That's why he often doesn't finish the one he started!" he whispers. Then he adds grumpily, "But he's always telling me to be patient."

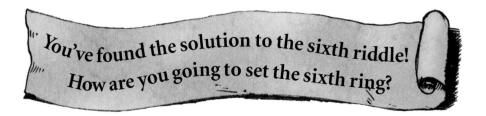

You've found the solution to the sixth riddle! How are you going to set the sixth ring?

THE PAINTER'S CONTEST

Salaì has made a good job of retouching the painting. But now the paint has to dry.

"Not long ago, one of the Master's paintings fell off the wall," he says, grinning.

Pablo's hackles stand up. But this time it's not Malfatto's fault. What? The great Leonardo made a mess of something? Is that possible?

Salaì lies on the floor, resting on his elbows.

"I'll tell you about it, but then you have to tell me something, too."

It's a deal.

"Well it all started when Leonardo was commissioned to paint a fresco in the Palazzo Vecchio in Florence," he begins. "It was a scene depicting the victory of the Florentines over the Milanese at the battle of Anghiari."

"Leonardo wasn't keen to do it because he learned that his biggest rival, Michelangelo, was going to paint a fresco on the opposite wall. He didn't really like Michelangelo and so he was determined that his fresco would be better."

"First of all he drew the design on paper. No fewer than 950 sheets of paper had to be glued together. It was then that the disaster occurred."

81

"The oil Leonardo used was bad and after he had painted part of it...

It was supposed to be an oil painting and Leonardo bought the materials for it: 30kg of Greek pitch, 75 kg of linseed oil, 225kg of gypsum as well as 16kg white lead, and 12kg of caustic soda, 311g of nut oil and a few sheets of gold leaf.

...the paint fell off the wall and then the plaster did too."

How did the contest between Michelangelo and Leonardo end?

Salaì laughs and waggles his feet, still wearing the shoes he took from you.

"Leonardo gave up. He went to Milan, where the French king had a commission for him. He's obliged to work for dukes and kings, because they pay good money."

And Michelangelo? Did he finish his work?

Salaì shakes his head, and his curls bob up and down.

"No, he didn't either. He didn't even start. The pope asked him to go to Rome. He was supposed to paint a chapel there – the Sistine chapel, that's what it's called."

So even great painters sometimes make mistakes.

The door to the studio opens and Alberto and the other painters return. A wiry man appears behind Alberto. His arms are covered in dough and when he pats his long apron, a cloud of white dust rises into the air.

"He stole three honey-buns last night!" he bellows, pointing at Salaì.

Salaì ducks his head.

"And then this morning he bought one from my wife, and he paid. Paid, with coins! He must have stolen them!"

Alberto grabs Salaì's ear "Go on, speak you little devil!"

As Salaì is pulled over to one side by his ear, coins fall out of his pocket and jingle on the floor.

"Where did you get the money from?"

"From the man with the pointed chin," he squeals.

From the man with the pointed chin? From Dr. Malfatto!

THE LITTLE DEVIL

Leonardo has come back into the studio.

"From the man with the pointed chin? What does he want you to do?" he asks sternly, with his hands pressed to his sides. He signals to Alberto to let go of Salaì, who stumbles and falls at Leonardo's feet.

"To ask the visitors for a coat," he whines, pointing at you and Pablo.

He obviously means a code, the Leonardo Code!

Sadly, Leonardo shakes his head.

"I'll never do it again!", Salaì promises and then calls in your direction,

"Please, don't be cross with me!"

Where is Dr. Malfatto? Where is he hiding?

You must find out because you need the **blue compass.**

Salaì is already back on his feet. He dusts off his torn trousers.

"I'll look for him. I'll find him. I promise. Honestly. I really will this time."

Can you trust him?

Before anyone can stop him, Salaì has gone.

Pablo gives you a quick look, blinks and then starts to follow him.

To be on the safe side he won't let Salaì go off on his own this time.

The waiting begins.

Time passes very slooooooooooooowly.

It must be midday – at least your tummy is rumbling and Leonardo brings you some bread and fruit – when Mr. Tonatelli awakes up. Stiffly he hobbles into the studio, his face wrinkled.

Still no news from Salaì and Pablo!

Mr. Tonatelli looks with interest at a drawing, which Leonardo has hung up.

"We all have a centre!" Leonardo explains.

What does he mean by that?

He points at the man's tummy button in the drawing.

"That is the centre of the circle!"

The man Leonardo has drawn fits exactly within the circle but also within the square.

"I have measured lots of people," Leonardo continues.

"From the top of the head to the bottom of the chin is exactly one tenth of the body height."

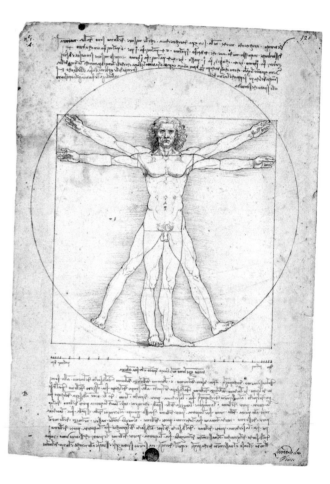

Is that really true? Measure it yourself!!

"And from the chest to the top of the head is exactly a quarter of what you measure from the toes to the top of the head."

Really? Take a tape measure and check.

85

"At the age of three, a child is half his or her adult height," Leonardo continues.

He gets a pile of drawings and spreads them out in front of you.

They all show people – naked people.

"I have to study the length of the limbs, the chest and the head very precisely," Leonardo says.

The relation of the body parts to one another is called proportions.
Proportions were very important to Leonardo.
When the proportions are right, the drawing is harmonious.

Only one of these pictures shows a person with the right proportions.

Which one is it?

The man with the outstretched arms.

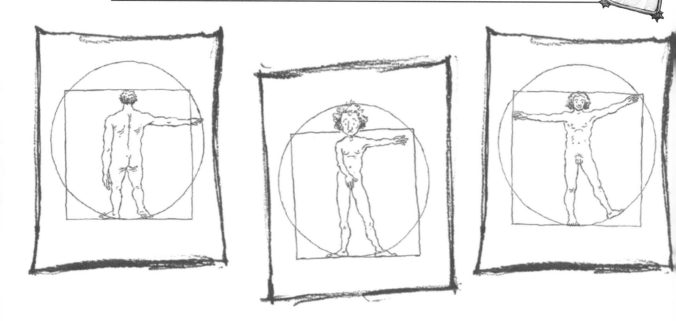

VERY MYSTERIOUS

Something very mysterious happens.
A visitor knocks at Leonardo's front
door. Leonardo opens it to see a man
wearing a monk's habit.
He has pulled the wide hood right over
his head, so his face is hidden by its shadow.
Without a word, the stranger hands Leonardo a wooden case. Then he turns
and strides off.

Surprise number one:

Leonardo opens the case and lifts out an object.

You've never seen it before, but you know immediately what it is.

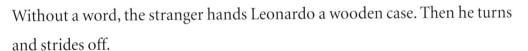

Surprise number two:

You suspect you know the identity of the hooded man.

But you can prove it too.

What is in the case and who is the man in the cloak?

It's Wallatto. You can see his shoes
peeping out beneath the cloak. And
he has brought the blue compass.

It must be a trap! There's no other explanation. Or is there?

Minutes later, Salaì and Pablo return. Pablo has his nose to the ground.

He's following Malfatto's scent, which has led him back to Leonardo's door.

Pablo barks and wags his tail with excitement.

He picks up the trail again and runs off down the alleyway, in the direction

Malfatto took when he left the house. When he reaches the river he loses

the scent.

The crook must have swum across. He's nowhere to be seen.

Where is Mrs. Bart hiding?

Why did Malfatto bring the **blue compass?**

How is he going to travel back from Leonardo's time to the present?

Or does he want to stay here?

Isn't he interested in opening the stone safe anymore?

What is his plan?

Endless questions!

Mr. Tonatelli confirms that the **blue compass** is genuine.

So long as Malfatto hasn't tampered with it and broken something, it should

work and you will be able to travel back to the present.

Has Malfatto really given up?

"We must open the stone safe and protect its contents from Malfatto,"

Mr. Tonatelli, tells you. It's clear from his voice that the situation is urgent

now.

"So we have to find the solution to the seventh riddle!"

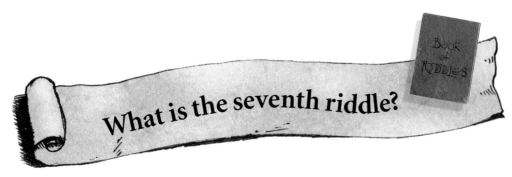

What is the seventh riddle?

Leonardo listens to the riddle and shakes his head. He has no idea what it means.

Tonatelli continues to give orders, "You and Pablo must take me back to the museum using the blue compass. Then, using the red compass , you can carry on looking for the solution. I will guard the safe – Malfatto can't be trusted."

Leonardo is sorry to say goodbye. He still had so many questions to ask you. Even Salaì secretly wipes tears from his eyes.

An icy blue flash erupts from the blue compass. It surrounds you and wallows you up like a hurricane.

A roar fills your ears. Then, like a spin-dryer slowing down, it becomes deeper and quieter.

You find yourselves back in entrance hall of the museum.

A breeze whistles between the pillars, then gradually fades away.

Mr. Tonatelli lets out a deep sigh of relief. Your task is now to travel back to different periods of Leonardo's life and research his greatest works of art!

Solve the seventh riddle! After Mr. Tonatelli has turned the precious stone on the red compass, he solemnly passes both compasses to you.

Pablo paws at your leg, until you pick him up. He's coming with you. Naturally!

THE GREATEST ARTIST

In a flash, the red compass transports you back to Leonardo's time.
You're in a town, in the centre of a large square. Pablo wriggles free and
jumps down onto the sandy ground.
People are standing in front of a massive statue of a horse, gazing at it
in admiration. It's huge, at least as tall as a two-storey house.
Two men are chatting nearby.

"So how long do you think Leonardo's statue will survive the wind and the weather? After all, the horse is only made of clay!" one says, in a nasal tone. "This is only a model," the other replies. "He's planning to cast the horse in bronze. But he can't at the moment because of the war. All the bronze is needed to make cannonballs."

"It's an accomplished work!" the first man adds.

"Yes, the horse is Master Leonardo's favourite animal," his companion agrees.

> **How do you say horse in Italian?**
> Cavallo

How embarrassing! Pablo has cocked his leg against one of the columns supporting the statue. When he notices your look of disapproval, he sticks his nose in the air as if to say, "Well what do you expect? I'm only a dog and I have to go sometime!"

But not up against this great work of art!

The solution to the seventh riddle cannot be found here though. As it says:

> "A great piece of art, oh what a shame!
>
> Ornament of a damp room once became,
>
> The room where it hung was at that time quite rare,"

This enormous horse couldn't possibly have hung anywhere. So you turn the red stone on the compass again.

To Leonardo's great disappointment the giant horse statue was not cast during his lifetime.

THE LAST SUPPER

The **red compass** transports you to a long, narrow room. You are stunned by the silence that greets you there. You are facing a wooden dining table with space for twenty people or more.

At one end of the room there's an opening halfway up the wall. Through it you can see another room where a second table is set up at right angles to the table next to you, like in a T-shape. You're alone in the room, but a small group of people has gathered in the room next door. The host is a bearded man. Men are sitting on either side of him, deep in conversation.

Wait a minute!

There is no other room! You're looking at a picture. It is painted directly onto the wall. The wooden ceiling above you carries on in the painting, giving the impression of looking into a second room.

Pablo has gone very quiet. He isn't even panting anymore. With his yellow paw, he points at a man on a ladder in front of the painting.

It's Master Leonardo. Without turning round, he points at a figure in the picture. It's a man without a face.

"I've searched the whole of Milan, but I still haven't found a suitable face for Judas, so I can't finish him."

A monk, wearing a brown habit, comes through the door. He's carrying a bowl of soup and bangs the edge of the bowl with a wooden spoon.

"Master Leonardo, you must eat something. You haven't even had a drink today! You can't carry on like this. Think of your health!"

The monk spots you. But not Pablo, he has found a few breadcrumbs, which he licks up greedily. When the monk sees your puzzled look, he walks over to you.

He isn't very old and his face beams with joy.

"Can you hear Jesus saying the words, too?" he whispers.

What does he mean?

"The fresco shows Jesus and his disciples at the moment when he says, 'Verily I say unto you, that one of you shall betray me.'"
Jesus' eyes draw you towards him like a magnet.
"Sometimes, when I stand in front of this painting, I feel like I'm floating," the monk says quietly. There's still a lot he could tell you.

The faces in the painting are those of well-known citizens of Milan. Leonardo even looked for models for the hands.

The lines of perspective meet in Christ's right eye. That is why the picture draws in the onlooker so eerily.

A king liked the painting so much that he wanted to own it and take it with him. This would have meant destroying the whole wall, so it stayed in the monastery in Milan.

Leonardo has identified the traitor at the table.
He's just knocking over the salt.
Spilled salt used to be a sign of great misfortune.
Where is the traitor sitting?

Third on the left from Jesus.

Leonardo gives a snort.

"The thumb. I can't remember what it looks like!" he mumbles, getting down from the ladder and rushing off. He's deep in thought and doesn't notice you or the monk – he didn't touch his soup either. He has to go and look at the hands.

The Last Supper might be the solution to the riddle or, then again, it might not. It's certainly great, but it's not hanging. It's painted on the wall.
It's time to move on.
Nothing happens when you turn the precious stone on the **red compass.** You can't push the stone in or pull it further out of the compass either.
Is it stuck? Something moves in your pocket. It pokes you, as if it wants to attract your attention. It must be the **blue compass.**

It is the **blue compass**! Beneath the domed glass, you recognise the Museum of Adventures and see Mr. Tonatelli, who is the size of a bean, waving at you. It must mean you're supposed to go back. Pick Pablo up, and turn the blue stone. But you'd better wait until the monk has left the room, otherwise, the poor boy will be completely confused.

MONA LISA'S SECRET

"All wrong! It must be the Mona Lisa!"

These are the words with which Mr. Tonatelli greets you. He charges off
through the museum using two upside-down brooms as crutches.

You and Pablo have trouble keeping up with him.

"I was only thinking of LARGE works," he explains, rushing on.

"But it must mean the most famous picture Leonardo ever painted."

You have arrived at the door of the Gallery of Living Paintings.

"Talk to her. I'm sure she can help you. I'll meet you at the stone safe!"

Pablo stands up on his back legs and leans against the red door.

It swings open at once. As soon as you are inside the gallery, it shuts
behind you.

Leaning heavily on the broomsticks, Mr. Tonatelli hurries towards the
Magic Gallery, intending to lock it. As he pulls the green door to, he glances
at Leonardo's portrait on the wall.

"Blasted bristle brush!" he exclaims. For a moment he feels as if someone is
trying to crush his heart. What he sees can only mean **one thing**!

He wants to warn you, but as he turns around, somebody blocks his way.

The Gallery of Living Paintings looks different somehow.

The floor and walls are yellowish-grey marble.

A small picture hangs in front of you. It looks tiny – no bigger than the
screen of a small television. The famous Mona Lisa smiles out at you.

Pablo barks at the painting. The Mona Lisa looks at you both and blinks. You really can ask her questions now.

Who are you?

"My name is Lisa del Giocondo. My husband is a rich merchant from Florence. It was he who asked Leonardo to paint my portrait."

How long did this painting take Leonardo?

"About four years. There aren't any sketches and there's not a single sentence about me in any of his notebooks."

Why is this picture so famous?

"There are many reasons – Leonardo always wanted his paintings to be as true to nature as possible.

People have said that it is so realistic you can see the arteries pulsating in my neck. Maybe I am also famous, because nobody has ever made a portrait look so alive before. As if you could see into my soul."

Why are you smiling so mysteriously?

"That's a secret between me and Leonardo!"

It looks as if it was misty when the picture was painted. Is that deliberate?

"Well done! Leonardo never painted hard lines between light and dark areas. There's always a transition. Like when it's misty or smoky.

This effect is called 'Sfumato', from the Italian word for 'smoke'. With this technique Leonardo ensured that there was no sharp contrast between the foreground and background, so objects look very realistic, rather than as if they're cut out and glued on."

The picture looks rather dark!

"Once the colour of my face was rosy, but the painting has darkened over the years."

> **From where does the light fall onto the Mona Lisa's face? You can find out by looking at the shadows.**
> From the top left.

The seventh riddle!
Does the Mona Lisa know the answer?

She listens attentively, when you read it to her. But instead of giving an answer, she just keeps on smiling mysteriously. She really is beautiful, but right now her smile is getting on your nerves.

Mr. Tonatelli is standing in front of the stone safe, waiting impatiently for you. Again and again he runs his hands over the grooves of the symbols, letters and signs engraved in the stone rings. He tries turning one of the rings. First there's a grating sound then, from inside the column, comes a heavy clicking noise.

Click - click - click – click.

Each click sounds the same. It's impossible to tell from the noise, which is the right position. He opens his mouth to shout something.

A sharp **Sssssssssssssst!** stops him.

In the Gallery of Living Paintings, the Mona Lisa says in a soft voice, "Let me tell you what's happened to me over the past five hundred years!" Pablo pricks up his ears.

"Leonardo never gave me away. When he went to France as an old man, I stayed with Salaì – who later sold me to the French King."

"I have hung on the walls of many palaces. But not just in noble drawing rooms, once I was used to decorate a bathroom!"

"Emperor Napoleon put me up in his bedroom.
And it was Napoleon who allowed me to be
exhibited in the famous Louvre in Paris.
You can still find me there."

"I have also been stolen. That was in 1911. An Italian
painter took me. But I was found and returned to my gallery
in the Louvre."

"I've been through some terrible things. Acid was poured
over me, and my lower part was destroyed. It took years
for skilled painters to restore me again."

"Today, I hang under thick unbreakable glass.
I'm not allowed to travel anymore.
Whoever wants to see me, has to visit me here."

"I have often been copied. But not always successfully!"

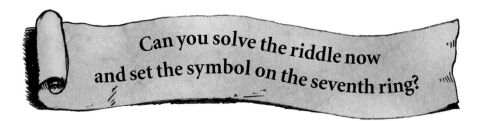

Can you solve the riddle now
and set the symbol on the seventh ring?

CRACK THE CODE!

Now you have all seven solutions!

At last! The stone safe can finally be opened!

As you leave the Gallery of Living Paintings, Pablo suddenly starts to bark loudly.

There's a metallic **click!**

Pablo puts his nose into the air and his tail starts to rotate. He darts off.

What's got into him?

Mr. Tonatelli is waiting in the dim room at the end of the corridor.

"Don't you have to go home?" he asks.

Home? Now?

His eyes flicker and he bends down as if he wants to whisper something confidential to you.

The naked light bulb dangles above him. There's still a cloud of dust in the air. It smells of old suitcases and leather.

A rustling sound comes from behind the pile of wooden boxes.

Probably a mouse.

Then you hear a yelp from one of the galleries.

What's happened to Pablo? After a short silence you hear him again.

He sounds terrified.

Mr. Tonatelli is staring over your shoulder through the door to the corridor.

Here comes Dr. Malfatto. He's carrying Pablo under his arm, like a set of bagpipes. He's holding the dog's mouth shut with his other hand. Pablo is trying to escape, but Malfatto's thin arms are stronger than they look.

"Jellybeans can be dangerous," he warns Pablo, as though it were all his fault.

The rustling from behind the boxes wasn't a mouse, but Mrs. Bart.

She's wearing her tight leather jacket again and is struggling to do the zip up.

"Put the code in!" she bellows at you. "And don't look at me like that. These jackets are always cut too tight. I'll give that tailor a piece of my mind."

But how did the two of them get back to the present?

"Get on with it!" Bart grunts. Behind you, Malfatto is squeezing the helpless Pablo even tighter. The little dog lets out a pitiful whimper. Bart turns to Dr. Malfatto and flutters her eyelashes.

"You've done it again doctor. I must congratulate you."

Malfatto has his eyes fixed on the stone safe.

"I haven't got what I want yet."

"It's only a matter of seconds!" She turns to you again, bares her teeth and snarls like a dog about to attack.

"Bart! More style!" Dr. Malfatto reminds her.

"I'm sorry, doctor," she says respectfully. Then she turns to you,

"The code! Otherwise this dog will be mincemeat."

You have no choice!

The stone rings feel ice cold.

You hear a crunching and cracking from inside the column.

It sounds like the cogs of a giant clock. Malfatto and Bart glare at the top tensely. As soon as you have turned the seventh ring, Mrs. Bart

makes a grab for it, with her sausage-like fingers.

"It won't move!" she cries.

Is the code wrong?

Here are the correct settings:

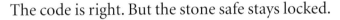

Lyre \ helicopter \ arm \ ermine \camera obscura\ shell \ bath

The code is right. But the stone safe stays locked.

"I'll strangle the little beast," Malfatto threatens coldly.

"Don't! Please don't! This must be one of my great-grandfather's tricks,"

Tonatelli says quickly, leaning heavily on the column.

He hobbles around it once.

There has to be a reason why it won't open!

You have seen the word before. Not long ago.

Could it be a hint to the true Leonardo Code?

Perhaps something else has to be adjusted on the stone safe?

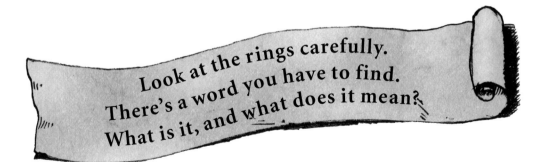

Look at the rings carefully.
There's a word you have to find.
What is it, and what does it mean?

Find the word!
The right code has something to do with it....

Tonatelli winks at you. You both know the solution: But how can you rescue Pablo without letting Malfatto get his hands on the contents of the safe?

"I'm going to count to three, then my patience will be at an end," Malfatto threatens.

"ONE!"

"Ha ha ha!" Mrs. Bart gives a mean laugh.

Pablo whimpers.

Mr. Tonatelli snorts like a stubborn horse and waves his checked handkerchief about.

You know the Leonardo Code. But what should you to do?

"Give me the **red compass**!" Mr. Tonatelli demands.

What does he want it for?

Tonatelli takes the golden egg. Bart looks at it scornfully.

Malfatto's eyes are now just narrow, mean slits.

"TWO!"

"You don't need that thing now!" Mrs. Bart hisses.

Reluctantly Mr. Tonatelli stretches out his hand with the **red compass** .

She snatches it from him.

The compass is already lying in her fat palm, when Tonatelli presses the red stone and quickly pulls his hand away.

The flash is brighter than the midday sun and you feel a wave of heat.

Dazzled, you have to close your eyes.

A terrified cry emerges from the centre of the light, and then dies away, like an express train speeding into a tunnel.

"Bart?" Malfatto calls, almost guiltily.

All that is left of the doctor's assistant are her footprints on the dusty floor.

"That's it. You've gone too far!" Malfatto snarls. He's going to hurt Pablo.

You have to do something!

Grab something to distract him.

Dr. Malfatto's lips contort into a mocking smile, when he sees what you're reaching for. Then he realises what a predicament he is in – he needs both hands to hold onto Pablo, so he can't snatch his spark-dagger back.

But you can throw him off balance with the broom. You just have to twist it between his feet and make him fall over, like Salaì did to you in the studio. Malfatto lets out a dreadful curse, and tries to use his arms to regain his balance. He drops Pablo and then tumbles to the ground. He squirms around like a lizard, but he can't get back on his feet.

With a deep growl Pablo jumps on his chest. He flashes his teeth and holds them threateningly close to Malfatto's neck. The crook lies on the floor, not daring to move a muscle.

Pablo's teeth are too close, and he's very angry.

"Mrs. Bart and Malfatto returned to the museum using the **blue compass**, then Bart stayed here.

Malfatto was able to return to Leonardo's time through the painting, and Mrs. Bart waited next to the picture to bring him back," Tonatelli explains.

So the doctor wanted to let you do all the work and to open the stone safe for him.

That's not going to happen though.

Half an hour later, the police pick up Dr. Malfatto.

"He attacked me!" Tonatelli tells them for the record.

When Malfatto is led away, you can hear him ranting to himself, "That fat slug messed it all up. Why did I choose her to do the dirty work? Pea brain!"

If only Mrs. Bart could hear what her boss thinks of her.

After the door has shut behind Malfatto and the police, you can finally turn your attention to the stone safe. The word, which is formed by the rings, is **CAVALLO** and this is the final clue. The Leonardo Code consists of the horse, which appears seven times – that is, on every ring.

Tonatelli's hands are trembling as he begins to adjust the rings. Horse after horse appears between the groove in the base and that in the top. When he turns the last one it clicks into place, a fierce whirlwind starts inside the safe. It creaks and rattles, cracks and clicks – it clatters like a long chain being dragged over a sheet of metal.

The top of the column starts wobbling gently, then loosens so you can lift it off with both hands. Pablo jumps onto the column and pokes his nose inside. He grabs something with his teeth, and pulls it out.

It's a brush!

A paintbrush?

Tonatelli is already leaning over the safe and reaches inside cautiously.

He feels around but all he finds is a leather scroll, tied by a leather cord.

The leather is protecting a piece of paper, on which something is written in mirror writing. It's Leonardo's handwriting. The message is from him!

Murmuring to himself, Tonatelli deciphers the words.

His eyes read the lines over and over again. Slowly he lowers the sheet. With immense respect he takes the brush from Pablo.

"Leonardo used this to paint the Mona Lisa. This document proves it. He wrote it himself!"

The brush must be worth a fortune.

"If I exhibit this, it will certainly attract a lot of visitors, and I'll be able to pay off my debts with the money from the tickets," Tonatelli tells you happily. "Or I could sell the brush. It's sure to fetch a high price."

Mr. Tonatelli is overjoyed. The brush means he can keep his house and his museum, as well as the Museum of Adventures, which only you know about. Carefully he wraps the brush in his checked handkerchief and strokes it like a baby. Indignant, Pablo scratches at Tonatelli's trouser leg.

"Now don't get jealous," his master says soothingly.

"See you soon!"

You're back outside. Pablo and Mr. Tonatelli, wave you off from the window.

"Thank you very much!" the owner of the museum calls after you.

Did all this really happen to you?

Or was it just a dream?

As you walk down the steps, something hard hits you in the back.

It must have been thrown from the roof.

Salaì is standing right by the stone gargoyles. He has flung your shoes after you. Magically, the red velvet suit you were wearing has disappeared, and there you are back in your own clothes again!

"Your shoes were too tight! They've given me blisters!" he complains. Then he grins broadly. "You're OK though!"

A second later, he's disappeared. Two cooing doves land on the spot where he was standing.

There's a strange sound at your feet. Pablo has run after you and his yelping sounds muffled because he's holding a familiar-looking piece of card in his mouth.

He scratches your leg and holds the ticket out to you.

Take it!

Then you can return to the Museum of Adventures.

You can certainly expect another exciting experience, for there are still many galleries and rooms to be discovered.

Pablo barks at you. It sounds, like:

"I'll be waiting for you!"

So, see you next time at the Museum of Adventures!

A note from the author:

Hello!

How did you like your visit to the **Museum of Adventures**? The idea came to me when I got lost in an old museum and discovered mysterious doors beyond which lay rooms that nobody ever entered.

Since I found out about the way Leonardo worked, I've always kept a notebook myself, and I can recommend it. It's fun to observe things, take notes and draw. Give it a try!

By the way, you will soon be able to enjoy a new adventure in Mr. Tonatelli's museum! I'm already writing it!

See you soon!

Thomas Brezina

In China, where his books have stormed the bestseller lists, Thomas Brezina is called 'master of adventures'. His aim is to fascinate and inspire children through his stories, and make reading a real adventure. His successful series of books, including: The Tiger Team series, Tips and Tricks for Junior Detectives have been published in more than 30 languages.

About the illustrator:

Laurence Sartin

has illustrated numerous books for children and young adults. He lives in France and Germany, where he teaches design and illustration at the Akademie Regensburg.

THE WORKS IN THIS BOOK

Cover, pages 97, 98, 100   Portrait of Lisa del Giocondo (Mona Lisa), 1503-1506 and later; Paris, Musée de Louvre

Pages 5, 12, 40   Study for an Aerial Screw, 1487-1490; Paris Bibliothèque de l'Institut de France

Page 16   Notes on the Position of a Bird's Wing in Relation to the Wind, 1505; Turin, Biblioteca Reale

Page 16   Notes on Changes of Direction during Flight, 1505; Turin, Biblioteca Reale

Page 16   Reflections and Studies of the Centre of Gravity of a Bird, 1505; Turin, Biblioteca Reale

Pages 18, 31   Head of a Bearded Man (Self Portrait) around 1510-1515; Turin, Biblioteca Reale.

Page 18   Vincent Van Gogh, Self Portrait with Bandaged Ear, 1889; London, Courtauld Institute Galleries

Page 18   Section from The Mozart Family by Johann Nepomuk della Croce, 1780/81; Salzburg, Mozarteum

Page 18   Albrecht Dürer, Self Portrait, 1500; Munich, Alte Pinakothek

Page 19   Pablo Picasso, Self Portrait, 1940; Cologne, Ludwig Collection

Page 19, 81   Daniele da Volterra, Michelangelo Buonarotti, around 1548-1553; Haarlem, Teylers Museum

Page 26   Head of Leda, around 1505-1510; Windsor Castle, Royal Library

Page 26   Profile of a Man in a Headdress, around 1485-1487; Windsor Castle, Royal Library

Page 26   Section of a Study for The Last Supper and Architectural Sketches around 1495; Windsor Castle, Royal Library

Page 26, 60   Section from Profiles of an Old Man and a Youth (Salaì?), around 1500-1505; Galleria degli Uffizi, Florence

Page 26   Head of a Young Woman, around 1488-1492; Windsor Castle, Royal Library

Page 34/35, 40   Study for a Flying Structure, 1489-90; Paris Bibliothèque de l'Institut de France

Page 39   Study of an Articulated Wing, around 1488-1492; Milan, Biblioteca Ambrosiana, Codex Atlanticus

Page 39   Sketch of a Ship, around 1490-1495; Milan, Biblioteca Ambrosiana, Codex Atlanticus

Page 39   Plan and Cross-sections of Town Houses with Raised Streets and a Bicycle, around 1487-1490; Paris Bibliothèque de l'Institut de France

Page 39   Studies of an Automobile, around 1478-1480; Milan, Biblioteca Ambrosiana, Codex Atlanticus

Page 39	Section from Design for a Plough and a Tank, around 1485-1488; London, British Museum
Page 39	Drawing of a Foot-powered Grain Mill, Codex Madrid
Page 40	Section from Sketches and Notes for a Flying Machine and Parachute around 1485-1487; Milan, Biblioteca Ambrosiana, Codex Atlanticus
Page 47	Section of the Anatomical Study of the Pronation and Supination of the Arm around 1509/10; Windsor Castle, Royal Librar
Page 60	Virgin and Child with St. Anne, around 1502-1513; Paris, Musée de Louvre
Page 60	Sections from Studies of the Christ Child and St. Anne around 1501-1510; Venice, Gallerie dell'Accademia
Page 60	Section from a Study of St. Anne, around 1501-1510; Venice, Gallerie dell'Accademia
Page 60	Section from the Study of the Right Sleeve of Mary, around 1501 or 1510/11; Paris, Musée de Louvre, Cabinet des Dessins
Page 60	Section from a Study of the Head of St. Anne around 1501-1510; Windsor Castle, Royal Library
Page 60, 94	Section from the Study of the Right Sleeve of St. Peter in the Last Supper, around 1495; Windsor Castle, Royal Library
Page 60, 94	Study of Clasped Hands (Hands of John), around 1495; Windsor Castle, Royal Library
Page 62	Madonna Benois, around 1478-1480; St. Petersburg, The Hermitage
Page 62	Portrait of Cecilia Gallerani (Lady with an Ermine) Czartoryski Collection, Muzeum Narodowe, Cracow
Page 62	St John the Baptist, around 151-1516; Paris, Musée de Louvre
Pages 62, 72	The Virgin of the Rocks (The Virgin with the Infant Saint John adoring the Infant Christ accompanied by an Angel), around 1495-1499 and 1506-1508; London, National Gallery
Page 72	Section of the Study of the Robe of a Seated figure, Front View, around 1475-1478; Berlin, Staatliche Museen zu Berlin – Preußischer Kulturebesitz, Kupferstichkabinett
Page 85	Proportions of the Human Figure (Vitruvian Man), 1485-1490; Venice, Gallerie dell'Accademia
Page 92	The Last Supper, around 1495-1497; Milan, Santa Maria delle Grazie, north wall of the Refectory

INSTRUCTIONS

(If you find this too difficult, ask an adult to help you!)

1. Cut out the roll and the 7 strips, which will form the rings, from the cover, following the dotted lines as closely as possible.

2. Making sure that the white side is facing downwards, pull the roll and the seven strips carefully backwards and forwards over the edge of a table, so that they curve inwards.

3. Stick the edges of the roll together with sticky tape, so that the printed sides match. (You may find this easier if you use paper clips to hold the ends in place while you stick the edges together.)

4. Stick the strips together with sticky tape to form rings, and slip them onto the roll. Look at the numbers on the roll. They have to correspond exactly with the numbers on the rings!

5. Finally, bend the tabs on the roll outwards, so the rings can't slip off.

   The two tabs marked with an arrow show where you should position the correct signs or symbols.

Have fun!